SHE CHANGES
EVERYTHING

SHE CHANGES
EVERYTHING

≫ Seeking the Divine on a Feminist Path ≪

LUCY REID

t&t clark

NEW YORK • LONDON

T & T Clark International
Madison Square Park, 15 East 26th Street, New York, NY 10010

T & T Clark International
The Tower Building, 11 York Road, London SE1 7NX

T & T Clark International is a Continuum imprint.

Unless otherwise indicated, biblical quotations are from the New Revised Standard Version Bible, copyright 1989, Division of Christian Education of the National Council of the Churches of Christ in the United States of America. Used by permission. All rights reserved.

Cover design: Laurie Westhafer

Library of Congress Cataloging-in-Publication Data

Reid, Lucy.
   She changes everything : seeking the divine on a feminist path / Lucy
Reid.
     p. cm.
   Includes bibliographical references and index.
   ISBN 0-567-02621-3 (hardcover) — ISBN 0-567-02631-0 (pbk.)
   1. Feminist theology. 2. God—Motherhood.   I. Title.
BT83.55.R395 2005
230'.082—dc22

                                     2005015642

Printed in the United States of America

05 06 07 08 09 10   10 9 8 7 6 5 4 3 2 1

FOR MY CHILDREN, TOM, KATE, AND BEN.
May the mother love of the Holy One
bless you and keep you
in her heart and mine.

AND IN MEMORY OF MY PARENTS:
Marjorie, whose faith kindled my own,
and John, whose unbelief started my quest.

CONTENTS

ACKNOWLEDGMENTS

THE GESTATION AND BIRTHING of this book was a challenging journey for me. I am deeply grateful to David, my beloved life partner, for his ceaseless love and encouragement through it all, and for his willingness to leave England and the traditional expectations of marriage and ministry so that I could find my voice and my way.

I am also immensely grateful for the circle of women in my life who have challenged, taught, guided, and cheered me on: Barb Quinlan, Amy Cousineau, Jean Wright, Melody Wren, Dawn Reynolds, Jane Buchan, Alison Jasper, the women of the Guelph goddess retreats and spirituality circles, those in my dream group, and my sisters—Joanna, Nikki, and Morag. You have shown me different faces of the Feminine Divine, and given me more than you can know. Thank you.

NON CREDO

I want to say No.
I want to stand up and proclaim
as boldly
as any believer
the creed of my unbelief.

I do not believe
in God as an almighty Father,
the King of kings and Lord of lords.

I do not trust in that God of power and might
for there is too much blood
on his hands.

He is the God of genocide;
the God of savage crusades
and holy wars.

He is the God who commands
perfect obedience.
Punishment, death and hell
are his weapons.

He is the Godfather God,
watching us from a distance
and judging all our deeds.

He allows immeasurable pain,
permits undeserved suffering
for reasons beyond our knowing.

His ways are inscrutable,
as far beyond us as heaven
from earth.

We are not worthy
to gather up the crumbs
under his table.

But I do not want those crumbs.
I decline the invitation to that table.
I do not believe in that God
and so I have to say No.

I will shout it and sing it.
I will weep it and pray it.
I will paint it on my walls
and wear it on my clothing.

And after a thousand years of saying No to him,

I will be ready

to say Yes

to you.

INTRODUCTION

WHAT HAPPENS TO TRADITIONAL mainline Christian theology and spirituality when we take seriously the insights of feminism? When God is "she," when we move beyond a Father God, what difference does it make? Over the last century women have become ordained leaders in some churches, and more recently the issue of inclusive language has appeared on the ecclesiastical horizon, but has anything changed more deeply? This book raises these questions, but begins with a voice of protest, a creed of unbelief, crying out "No!" to the old order.

Coming to No, arriving at a point where protest is the only option, is a vital staging post on the pilgrimage of faith. This is particularly true, in my experience, for women raised in a patriarchal religion such as Christianity where the language and theology have been determined almost totally by men. As women we are socialized to agree or adapt, so many of us have sat quietly in our churches mentally disagreeing with what is being said or done but rarely finding the words or the ways through which to challenge it. We are adept at translating, reinterpreting, or ignoring what does not fit. We tell ourselves that although God is called Father that does not make God male. We have serious reservations about religion as we know it, but we send our children to Sunday school and sit in the pews more faithfully than our menfolk, because there is nowhere else to go. But at some point the gulf between our external practice and our internal discomfort becomes too wide, and something has to give. Faith either ceases to be a personal experience, as we cave in to what is expected of us and smother our doubts, or we get off the bus and stand at the staging post of No.

The place of protest is not an easy place to be. It is painfully negative. It offends or hurts others, often those close to us, who are dismayed at our anger and afraid of our changes. And it does not furnish us with the answers we are seeking; we are likely to be more aware of what we have left than of what we can turn to in its place.

Coming to No precedes coming to know. It is a place of transition, with all the awkwardness and uncertainty of that.

But the turning point of No on the pilgrimage of faith has the power to clear the ground and fuel the engine. After the sapping experience of keeping silent, swallowing protest, repressing anger, protest is energy and movement. It excites. It is the stamp of the foot on the ground that announces, "Here I am! This is what I have to say! And if I can't find the words, here I am anyway!" And then the journey has direction and purpose, and the staging post becomes a launchpad, not a place to stay forever.

There may be several places of No along the way. Typically, we arrive at them without warning. They are unexpected but unmistakable. Once I was on retreat at a Christian spirituality center. I was not conscious of wrestling more than usual with my discomfort at the theology expressed in the worship services I was attending. But suddenly, in the midst of a celebration of the Eucharist, I could bear it no longer. The masculine language, the congregational passivity, the images of God as distant and mighty, the assumption of human sinfulness—it was all that and more. An inner elastic seemed to have reached its limit and snapped. I walked out of the chapel, hurried down the corridor, and then fled from the building, until I was running through the open grounds shouting my No to the apple trees. It was a powerful and personal exodus. There was no need then to nail my theses of protest to the door in Reformation fashion. It was enough that I had heard my own voice saying No, and felt my own legs carrying me out of there.

As a woman in the church, and as a priest, learning to say No and listening to what that means has been vital to my journey. Without the process of exodus, protest, dismantling, and revisioning, the Yes to God that is at the heart of faith would, for me, have been blurry and compromised. So I want to say No to the distortions of Christianity in its traditional patriarchal form, in order to say Yes to the faith that is emerging for me along a feminist path.

This is not a book just for women or feminists, although it does focus on the feminist path of spirituality and theology as I understand it. Rather, my hope is that this book might give voice to a melody that is in a different key from mainline Christian belief. It is a melody that has been drowned out by the strident tones of dogmatism and patriarchy, and by the cacophony of religious conflict, judgmentalism, and violence.

My choice of strong language is deliberate, because I am painfully aware of the harm that has been done in the name of religion. For example, when Christians have taught that God is an all-powerful Father and punishing judge, fear of this terrifying deity has crippled the hearts of believers. Fear and guilt, indeed, have been the common currency in missionary work for too much of the history of the church. Similarly, when Christians have proclaimed that Christ is the only way to salvation, and that hell awaits those who do not profess this faith, intolerance has violated the lives of many and spawned wars and atrocities. Even the more subtle violations have taken their toll. Doctrines of God's reigning beyond the world in heaven and of God's plan to end the world violently at the second coming of Christ some time in the future have made Christianity an "otherworldly" religion that denigrates this earthly world and sees it as an inanimate resource to be used and thrown away.

Liberal Christianity has distanced itself from these views, but has failed to offer a deeply convincing alternative. The fault lines continue to lie beneath the sophisticated surface. Instead, it has been the gifts of feminist theological thought that have enabled me to strip away the destructive aspects of the faith in which I was raised.

My roots are traditionally Christian, but my growth has branched out into fresh air. As a woman denied ordination by the Church of England because of my gender, I was in some way placed beyond the pale. Finding myself there, I explored the terrain and found questions, injustices, doubts, and alternative paths. When ordination became possible I was not the same. I had discovered feminist theology, questioned the "faith of our fathers," lost my belief in God and found it again renewed and transformed. My core images had changed: God was no longer almighty Father but could be compassionate Mother or birthing Spirit; Jesus was not God come down to earth from heaven, but my brother revealing the face of the Divine in us all; and salvation was not redemption from damnation but healing from brokenness.

For ten years I worked in parish ministry and incubated these images. But my roots in tradition became less and less able to nourish me, and my placement within traditional church settings was increasingly out of step with my inner foundations. I felt I was upholding traditions and beliefs that were at best outmoded and at worst damaging. And I was acutely aware of the general exodus societally from mainline organized religion. It was no longer meeting people's needs or articulating people's experience, pain, and hope.

A move to ministry on a university campus in a multifaith context enabled me to put down new roots. Now on the margins of church life, I felt freer to explore alternative ways of expressing my faith and offering my ministry. The self-censoring could stop. Instead of pruning a theological bonsai tree of orthodoxy by cutting off every piece of new growth, every budding of a challenging thought, I was able to let ideas, experiences, and reflections unfold and develop freely, in an environment dedicated in principle to the pursuit of knowledge by rigorous questioning.

In campus ministry my focus was now on those outside the church, with their skepticism and challenges to faith. In study groups, class discussions, residence talks, and individual conversations I discovered that the students' questions and stumbling blocks had been mine. Their cynicism with religion but thirst for spirituality was achingly familiar to me. Many, in rejecting traditional or popular Christianity, had had nothing with which to replace it and were spiritually beached.

Many, faculty and staff as well as students, were searching for a God they could believe in.

This book is for those searchers. It is for Alison, with her penetrating critique of religious hypocrisy, and for Kathy, in her lonely pilgrimage since she left the church. It is for Jack, who heard me speak and told me that his hope had been restored. And it is for my children, Tom, Kate, and Ben, that they may grow up with the courage and honesty to explore faith, test it, shape it, and make it their own.

This is not a textbook in feminist theology so much as a chronicle of my own journey and an excursion through the writings of others whose thought has been pivotal for me. For those who choose to read more widely, I include notes at the end of each chapter indicating my sources. In the first chapter, "Discovering the Feminine Face of God," I describe my research into the use of feminine imagery for God in the Bible and in Christian history, which I undertook while at theological college (seminary) in England. I was preparing for ministry as a deaconess—the closest I could come to ordination as a priest at that time—while the traditional all-male priesthood was being maintained. Similarly, academic theology was almost entirely the work of men, and the liturgical language for God in hymns, prayers, sermons, and creeds was exclusively masculine. Discovering the feminine face of the Divine was for me an affirming and exciting process, with radical implications. It undermined the tired old argument used against the ordination of women, which held that priests represent Jesus who was male and who came from a God revealed as Father, so that masculinity is an essential aspect of priesthood—and an implied attribute of God. It opened new paths of imagery and understanding that linked women's lives to the Divine and named women's reality as holy.

In the second chapter, "Searching for the Goddess," I summarize the work of two female scholars, Merlin Stone and Riane Eisler, whose studies of prehistoric Goddess-worshiping cultures gave me a fascinating insight into the time when, as Stone puts it, "God was a woman." Existing for thousands of years, these cultures make the Judeo-Christian culture appear in a very different light. For the first time I was able to see how it had been shaped by human forces, not ordained by God. The roles of men and women, the place of war, the stratification of society, the religious practices—none could be taken for granted any longer. With the hypotheses and imagination of feminist scholars, it became possible to envision a culture, society, and religion governed by peaceful partnership rather than hierarchical dominance. By stepping outside the assumptions of my own faith in my search for a God I could love, I encountered the many faces of the Goddess from past times and different cultures. I found them not alien but ancient, not outdated and irrelevant to the modern Western world but life affirming and much needed. Combining the wisdom of the Goddess with that of the God I had known, I reached toward a more whole image of the Divine, the Holy One who transcends all our language and knowledge.

But questioning one's faith, identifying its inadequacies, and exploring other paths is not a comfortable experience. So in the third chapter, "Loss of Faith: Rethinking," I write of the painful process of letting old beliefs die or—as often happens—struggling to keep them on life support when they are effectively already dead. An omnipotent God in heaven, who is ruler of the universe and who determines our lives on earth according to a mysterious plan, is often the God who becomes terminally ill for questers. This God is well known, but less and less believable. We outgrow this God, as we outgrew Santa Claus, or he drifts out of our lives as a vague abstraction that has ceased to have meaning. Sometimes we have to walk determinedly away without looking back, swallowing our tears and knowing that we have to move on. To lose faith in the God we used to know, without the hope that there is anything else, is to enter a barren agnosticism. We can no longer recite the creed of our past along with the faithful, but neither do we have an alternative creed.

My own experience was one of being pushed out of the security of my faith into periods of doubt, confusion, and reexamination. And it was the writings of feminist theologians and other nontraditional thinkers that led me to a reconstructed faith. Specifically, I encountered images of God as immanent, dwelling not beyond us but with us and within all of creation; as vulnerable and passionate; as laboring constantly to bring new life and goodness to birth. These were very different from the images I had grown up with and struggled to make sense of, especially when the problem of innocent suffering begged enormous questions of God's almighty power and infinite love. A God endlessly engaged in the costly process of creation, intimately close to us, sharing our pain, is markedly different from a majestic God who created the world once, long ago, and reigns over it now from a distance.

Sin and salvation, key concepts within the Christian faith, had also become problematic for me. Chapter 4, "Freedom: Sin, Salvation, and Liberation," explores the classical understanding of sin as wrongdoing, causing separation from God and bringing on humanity's head the penalty of eternal death, with salvation as the remedy for this fate through the death of Jesus. I found the implications of this theology intolerable, for it portrays God as legalistic or even sadistic, it reduces sin to law breaking—with an emphasis on the sin of pride as fundamental—and it views those outside the Christian fold as lost.

Liberation theology and feminist theology reframed sin and salvation for me, putting them within a context of a love relationship between God and humanity, not a trial. At a time when I badly needed a strong sense of self and courage to challenge the status quo in the church, I encountered a theology that did not stress passive obedience and submission to God's will but love for God's desire to bring justice to fruition. Salvation became liberation and healing, so that life could be lived fully, in relationships of equality. It was with enormous relief that I laid aside the bloody doctrines of Jesus' death as a sacrifice to atone for the sins of the world—slaughterhouse theology, as it has crudely but aptly been called.

The fifth chapter, "Wilderness: Letting Go," emerged from my experience of departing from mainline Christianity and living in the unmarked place of not knowing, traveling alone, letting go of security. There have been times when I have felt very alone, and wondered what faith I had left. The desire to run back to safety and certainty, closing the door to doubt, has been strong. At those times it was a gift and an encouragement to read of the similar journeys of others—mystics and poets, women and men. The Buddhist teaching of nonattachment became important to me, as did the Jungian insights into the Shadow, our rejected or hidden self, and our need to embrace it. I began to see traditional Christianity as obsessed with the light and fearful of darkness, death, and mystery. I found great wisdom in the hospice movement, which befriends death, and in earth-based spiritualities such as Wicca, which is holistic and unitive in its approach. A feminist perspective can integrate all of these voices of alternative wisdom and honor them as holy.

A unitive path, a faith which does not divide everything into dualistic sets of opposites (heaven and hell, sacred and secular, divine and human, good and evil), a spirituality which integrates both lived experience and received wisdom—these are the hallmarks of a religion I can follow. In chapter 6, "Ecofeminism: The Spiral of Life," I outline the holistic nature of a faith which rejects the forces that have abused and exploited nature, oppressed women and children, enslaved classes and nations. My exposure to feminism during the debate over the ordination of women occurred at the same time as my exposure to antimilitarism during the debate over nuclear weapons. Significantly, many of the women at Greenham Common in England, who set up a protest camp outside a military base housing nuclear arms, were also environmentalists and feminists. The global issues concerning peace, ecological well-being, and equality for all are inextricably linked together. Christianity, however, has been successfully used for centuries to keep women under the authority of men, to justify bloody wars, and to plunder the earth of its resources. The chapter examines why this has happened and how theology can be reframed to be life sustaining, earth honoring, and peacemaking. Feminists have been engaged in the work of reweaving the broken, divided strands into a strong web, where the Divine can be named as Gaia, the sustaining energy of all life.

Where does this leave me? Am I so far out on a limb from my Christian roots that the branch can no longer support me? In the final chapter, "Interfaith: Widening the Circle of Wisdom," I describe the ways in which non-Christian faiths have touched me and taught me, and I suggest a deeper form of ecumenism than mere religious tolerance. It is a form that cultivates openness to all sources of wisdom, encourages humility and self-criticism in every faith, and, most importantly, enables the individual to take responsibility for her own spiritual life. While I have serious reservations about much of Christianity as it exists in its institutional, traditional forms, Jesus Christ continues to be the human face of the Divine for me. He inspires me, guides me, challenges me. In him I see the passionate love of God, the healing power of God, the intimate, vulnerable presence of God. I do not call Jesus my Lord, because I can no longer use the language of hierarchy and dominion. I do not believe that he alone reveals God, because Buddhism, Judaism, Hinduism, aboriginal spirituality, and the religions of the Goddess have also enabled me to know the Divine more profoundly, and live in her way more wholly. I continue to approach other faith groups not in order to convert them to Christianity, but that we all might learn and grow.

Writing this book has been a process of giving voice and shape to my own journey of faith. When I began, during a sabbatical from my university ministry in the summer of 1998, I was afraid of where it might lead me. It was as though I had decided to parachute out of the safety of a plane and was unsure whether I would break my legs on landing, or find myself in hostile territory. Sometimes I wondered if I would disappear off the map altogether. I knew I would be articulating thoughts and ideas I had previously kept largely to myself and that I recognized were controversial and unorthodox. I was afraid that if I wrote honestly and personally I would be rejected by my colleagues and superiors, and even by some friends.

In fact the experience has been overwhelmingly life giving. After the long gestation period of two decades of reading, working, questioning, and wrestling, the writing has been like giving birth. And there can be no going back. A child cannot be unborn once she has entered the world. At times, as I found the words to convey my thoughts, and as I encountered those thoughts crystallized and sharp on the page as though for the first time, I imagined the voice of the reformer Martin Luther: "Here I stand; I can do no other." I can no longer remain silent about the abuses and madness within Christianity. I cannot pretend to believe what no longer makes sense. I will not let my faith be defined by others.

My hope is that this book, which is partly theological and partly autobiographical, will resonate with those who are on similar journeys beyond traditional Christianity. I hope it might offer an alternative framework of faith for those who know what they have given up believing but are less sure what they can retain. I hope it will encourage others to ask their own questions and explore where the Spirit leads.

During our sermon classes at theological college we were taught to use personal examples to illustrate our points, because what is the most personal is also the most general; others can identify with our stories. I still believe that to be true. I have read stories, particularly other women's stories, which have moved me to tears by their ability to touch my soul and give words to my pain and joy. So I am losing my academic discomfort about speaking in the first person in this book. It is impossible for me to write it objectively and dispassionately because it comes not just from my head but from my heart, gut, and soul. Similarly, I hope it will not be read dispassionately but engaged with and used as a springboard in the quest for the Divine.

The final chapter of the book, "Prayers for the Pilgrimage," is a collection of psalms and prayers I have written at different points along the journey. I offer them for use without condition. May they give voice to what others feel and know.

CHAPTER 1
Discovering the Feminine Face of God

THE CHURCH OF ENGLAND'S refusal to allow women to be ordained as priests led to my discovery of the feminine face of God. I had graduated from the University of Durham, England, with a degree in theology in 1978, after sensing some five years earlier a vocation to the priesthood. The Anglican Communion worldwide was rocking with conflict over the issue of women's admission to holy orders. In the United States the doors had been opened and women were being ordained, while in England and elsewhere the theological debates and organizational motions were still dominated by the voices opposed to women priests. Of all the arguments used to uphold a male priesthood, the central one appeared to be that since priests represented Christ who was male, who referred to God as his Father, and who chose twelve men to be his disciples, then his representatives should be male.

I remember attending a regional church meeting where the issue of the ordination of women was to be discussed. I was still an undergraduate at the time, and a supportive priest had invited me to share my views with the group. I spoke for a few minutes, using what I considered to be uncontroversial examples from the New Testament of Jesus being inclusive of women and of God being beyond gender. Self-consciously and nervously I sat down and waited for the discussion to begin. An elderly priest stood up, waved his hand dismissively, and said, "Bosh! It's all bosh!" I have no memory of who else spoke, or what else was said, just that wave of the hand and that effortless dismissal without discussion or engagement. I shrank inwardly to the stature of a foolish small child.

But with the optimism and resilience of youth I felt sure that the Church of England would eventually come to a more reasoned position and permit me and women like me to be ordained. Meanwhile I married David, a fellow theology graduate and ordinand, and—through the foresight of an enlightened principal who was prepared to risk opening his college to women—I began studies for ordination at the previously all-male domain of Ripon College Cuddesdon, Oxford.

While at Cuddesdon, as the debate continued both within the Anglican Church and between students at the college, I began to consider more seriously the theological arguments put forward. In particular, the question of the essential maleness of Jesus and the implied maleness of God unsettled me. On the one hand, it was stated as self-evident that God is neither male nor female but beyond gender. Yet on the other, Jesus' maleness and God's fatherhood were declared essential to a right understanding of the faith.

Like all cradle Christians of my generation and before, I had grown up in a religious tradition that used exclusively masculine pronouns for God: *he, his, him*. I continued to use them myself; there was no thinkable alternative. Intellectually I knew that God was not a male. Subconsciously, however, I had absorbed a decidedly masculine image of God, an image parodied by theologian Mary Daly as "Yahweh and Son incorporated."[1]

As a first tentative step out of the Christian theological mainstream, I decided to write a paper on the motherhood of God as part of my studies. I wanted to research any references in the Bible to God as maternal or motherlike, and to discover whether these images had been used in Christian spirituality in the past, and to what effect. Feminist theology was emerging at that time, chiefly in the United States, but it was a marginal discipline, either ignored or considered part of the lunatic fringe and rejected as the work of bra-burning, men-hating viragos. I did not consider myself to be a feminist at that time. In fact I was struggling to be accepted as "one of the boys," and was at pains to demonstrate that I was not aggressive or threatening in any way. The intent of my paper was innocent. I had no idea that it would be the beginning of a life-changing journey. In looking for a motherly God I stepped off the cliff and began to free-fall.

The Feminine Face of God in the Bible

The Hebrew and Christian scriptures contain a multiplicity of images for the Divine. When Moses, in Exodus 3, asks what God's name is, the answer is an enigmatic "I am who I am," or "I will be who I will be." God is being. The Hebrew avoidance of naming or depicting God sprang from a knowledge that the Divine is ultimately beyond our comprehension, our labeling, our defining. A plethora of images for God, then, underscores the belief that no single image is adequate.

So God is described in the Bible as a rock, shield, fortress; an eagle, lion, fire; the Ancient of Days; Alpha and Omega; a shepherd, potter, goldsmith; a king, judge, warrior. Images were drawn from daily life, the political order, and religious experience. Among these, however, I found female images for God, both overt and implicit: God as mother, midwife, woman in labor, wisdom woman (Sophia), mother bird, housewife, compassionate womb.

This glimpse of the feminine face of God was fleeting, vestigial, but unmistakable. The images are far outnumbered by the more familiar masculine images of God, but they are nonetheless deeply significant for what they contribute. Feminist theology seeks to turn the glimpse into a revelation, the whisper into a voice. It engages in a form of textual archaeology, digging through the layers of tradition where the masculine voice is the norm, to find the thin vein of feminine insight that has been hidden, distorted, lost, or ignored.

Theologian Elisabeth Moltmann-Wendel has written: "The idea of God is conceived mainly in masculine terms: male leadership roles are used to describe what God does. . . . What God is corresponds to what men would like to be—judge, king, ruler, army commander. In the process women's experiences . . . have been forgotten."[2] The uniquely female physical experiences of pregnancy, labor, childbirth, and breast-feeding can also be used to describe what God does and who God is. It is for that reason that the biblical authors used them. Motherhood as a powerful metaphor for divine activity and being is a part of our scriptural tradition. Yet it has all but been lost from sight.

God as Mother

I was a young woman still several years away from the birth of our first child when I found and studied the biblical references to God as mother, but they struck me like a shock wave slowly rippling through my being. I had not known they were there. No one had shown me this face of God. It was an intense, vulnerable face which seemed more intimate than the majestic face of Almighty God, the heavenly Father. I found it in Isaiah where I read of God's passionate concern for Israel expressed as the racking pains of a woman in labor:

> For a long time I have held my peace,
>> I have kept still and restrained myself;
> now I will cry out like a woman in labor,
>> I will gasp and pant. (Isa 42:14)

I saw it again when God's faithful love was likened to a mother's love for her child:

> Can a woman forget her nursing child,
>> or show no compassion for the child of her womb?
> Even these may forget,
>> yet I will not forget you. (Isa 49:15)

And the image is carried flexibly through a passage describing the restoration of Jerusalem:

> Rejoice with Jerusalem, and be glad for her,
>   all you who love her;
> rejoice with her in joy,
>   all you who mourn over her—
> that you may nurse and be satisfied
>   from her consoling breast;
> that you may drink deeply with delight
>   from her glorious bosom.
>
> For thus says the LORD:
> I will extend prosperity to her like a river,
>   and the wealth of the nations like an overflowing stream;
> and you shall nurse and be carried on her arm,
>   and dandled on her knees.
> As a mother comforts her child,
>   so I will comfort you;
>   you shall be comforted in Jerusalem. (Isa 66:10–13)

The psalmist uses similar mother-child language:

> But I have calmed and quieted my soul,
>   like a weaned child with its mother;
>   my soul is like the weaned child that is with me. (Ps 131:2)

These maternal images from the Bible became profoundly important to me. Perhaps because my own mother was a strong and gentle woman with a depth of love that I knew I could depend on, the motherly face of God removed at last any fear I had. Overzealous evangelical Christian friends of mine had spoken of hell awaiting those who were not saved. God had a harsh, unyielding side which could banish a lost soul to eternal punishment. He was a "Wait-till-your-father-gets-home" God, inspiring not trust but trepidation. A motherly God, by contrast, imaged as giving birth, breast-feeding, rocking, and comforting could be trusted to love without violence, without end.

Like the psalmist, the prophet Hosea depicts God as tenderly caring for the people of Israel and Ephraim in just such a maternal way, denouncing the people's faithlessness and rejection but nevertheless unable to countenance their destruction because of the visceral connection that deeply bonds them with God:

> When Israel was a child, I loved him,
>> and out of Egypt I called my son.
> The more I called them,
>> the more they went from me;
> they kept sacrificing to the Baals,
>> and offering incense to idols.
>
> Yet it was I who taught Ephraim to walk,
>> I took them up in my arms;
>> but they did not know that I healed them.
> I led them with cords of human kindness,
>> with bands of love.
> I was to them like those
>> who lift infants to their cheeks.
>> I bent down to them and fed them. . . .
>
> How can I give you up, Ephraim?
>> How can I hand you over, O Israel? . . .
>
> My heart recoils within me;
>> my compassion grows warm and tender.
> I will not execute my fierce anger;
>> I will not again destroy Ephraim;
> for I am God and no mortal,
>> the Holy One in your midst,
>> and I will not come in wrath. (Hos 11:1–4, 8–9)

The bond of God with God's people is thus not merely covenantal or even parental, but is described as maternal: from Deuteronomy in the Hebrew Scriptures to the Epistles of the Christian Scriptures we find references to God's giving birth to us:

You were unmindful of the Rock that bore you;
you forgot the God who gave you birth. (Deut 32:18)

In fulfillment of his own purpose he gave us birth by the word of truth, so that we would become a kind of first fruits of his creatures. (Jas 1:18)

Those who have been born of God do not sin, because God's seed abides in them; they cannot sin, because they have been born of God. (1 John 3:9)

This last passage suggests that God's children share in the very essence of God, with the seed of God within them. And it echoes a verse from Genesis, where the story of creation is told:

> In the beginning when God created the heavens and the earth, the earth was a formless void and darkness covered the face of the deep, while the spirit of God swept over [literally, "brooded over," like a bird on its nest] the face of the waters. . . .
>   Then God said, "Let us make humankind in our image, according to our likeness. . . ."
>   So God created humankind in the divine image,
>   in the image of God they were created;
>   male and female God created them. (Gen 1:1–2, 26–27; altered for inclusiveness)

Although easily lost in translation, the image here is of God's spirit as a brooding (maternal) presence in the dark watery chaos before light and life were spoken into existence. It is a womblike picture, with traces of the myths from ancient cultures that told of life emerging from a cosmic egg.[3] More significantly, when God creates human beings it is clear that both male and female are in the divine image. This has enormous theological implications for women, in contrast to Paul's statement that a man "is the image and reflection of God; but woman is the reflection of man" (1 Cor 11:7).[4] Many theologians from Paul to the present have assumed that men have a natural superiority over women, and have pointed to the alternative creation story in Gen 2 as proof, where Eve is created as an afterthought from Adam's rib, not from the dust of the earth and the breath of God as Adam was, and where she is created to be Adam's helper in a subordinate role. The Gen 1 creation story, however, tells of creation of male and female at one and the same moment, both "in the image of God," both blessed and rejoiced in by God as "very good" (Gen 1:27–28a, 31).

Interestingly, the Hebrew word for "God" in the first creation story is *Elohim*, a plural word originating from a feminine root.[5] The word implies that male and female are contained within the Godhead, which is the source of both but transcends each. We have no equivalent word for God in the English language, with the exception perhaps of the word "Trinity" with its implication of plurality. But just as the Trinity has become a triad of masculine roles (Father, Son, and Holy Spirit-he), so *Elohim* in translation becomes "God-he," and the subtle suggestion of both maleness and femaleness within the Divine is lost.

God as Midwife

Closely connected to the image of God as mother is that of God as midwife. God both gives birth and attends those giving birth, bringing new life into the world and caring intimately for it:

> It was you who took me from the womb;
>> you kept me safe on my mother's breast.
> On you I was cast from my birth,
>> and since my mother bore me you have been my God.
> (Ps 22:9–10)

In God's speech to Job from the whirlwind, the language of attending a birth is used:

> Who shut in the sea with doors
>> when it burst out from the womb?—
> when I made the clouds its garment,
>> and thick darkness its swaddling band. . . ? (Job 38:8–9)

In Isaiah's prophecy of Zion's deliverance, the metaphor again becomes that of delivering a child from the womb:

> Before she was in labor
>> she gave birth;
> before her pain came upon her
>> she delivered a son.
> Who has heard of such a thing?
>> Who has seen such things?
> Shall a land be born in one day?
>> Shall a nation be delivered in one moment?
> Yet as soon as Zion was in labor
>> she delivered her children.
> Shall I open the womb and not deliver?
>> says the LORD;
> shall I, the one who delivers, shut the womb?
>> says your God. (Isa. 66:7–9)

The metaphor of midwife invites images of God intimately connected to the human struggle for life and creativity. A midwife works with the laboring woman, coaching her, encouraging her, breathing with her. She is there through the long hours of blood, sweat, and tears, and she shares in the mess. A God like this is not aloof from us or in control of the events of our lives but alongside us. In our times of pain and confusion this midwife God keeps her eyes fixed on us and shows us how to get through. And when we bring forth the new life within us, she receives it with infinite tenderness and care. She delivers us.

God as Womb

Intriguingly, the Hebrew word for compassion, a characteristic attribute of God, derives from the word for womb. God's love is womblike.[6] Once again the implication is that such love is constant, merciful, tender. A classic verse from the Hebrew Scriptures that spells out the nature of God's compassionate love is Jer 31:20:

> Is Ephraim my dear son?
>   Is he the child I delight in?
> As often as I speak against him,
>   I still remember him.
> Therefore I am deeply moved for him [literally, "My womb trembles
>   for him"];
> I will surely have mercy on him,
>   says the LORD.

As a womb sustains and nurtures new life, and delivers it forth, so God's love nourishes and protects us, bringing us to fullness of being and maturity. Further, the love of the one who gives birth for the one who is birthed is so strong that nothing can finally intervene and destroy it. God is mother, womb, and midwife for us. Nothing can separate us from such love.

God as Sophia: The Wisdom Woman

Within the Bible is a body of writings known as the Wisdom literature.[7] It includes the books of Proverbs, the Wisdom of Solomon, and Sirach. Written to teach people how to live wisely in accordance with God's will, in this literature wisdom is often personified as a woman, named *Sophia* in Greek. She is depicted as a beautiful, pure, and noble woman who calls people away from the folly of arrogance, greed, and ungodliness to the wisdom of prudence, righteousness, justice, and understanding.

Sophia speaks of God as a separate being from herself, and as her creator, and yet her words suggest that she is more than God's creation; she is herself a manifestation of the Divine, coexisting and cocreating with God:

> The LORD created me at the beginning of his work,
>   the first of his acts of long ago.

Ages ago I was set up,
> at the first, before the beginning of the earth. . . .

> When he established the heavens, I was there,
> > when he drew a circle on the face of the deep,
> when he made firm the skies above, . . .

> when he marked out the foundations of the earth,
> > then I was beside him, like a master worker;
> and I was daily his delight. (Prov 8:22–23, 27–30)

When Sophia is described in the Wisdom of Solomon, her attributes are clearly divine rather than creaturely:

> There is in her a spirit that is intelligent, holy,
> unique, manifold, subtle,
> mobile, clear, unpolluted,
> distinct, invulnerable, loving the good, keen,
> irresistible, beneficent, humane,
> steadfast, sure, free from anxiety,
> all-powerful, overseeing all,
> and penetrating through all spirits
> that are intelligent, pure, and altogether subtle.
> For [Sophia] is more mobile than any motion;
> because of her pureness she pervades and penetrates all things.
> For she is a breath of the power of God,
> and a pure emanation of the glory of the Almighty;
> therefore nothing defiled gains entrance into her.
> For she is a reflection of eternal light,
> a spotless mirror of the working of God,
> and an image of [God's] goodness.
> Although she is but one, she can do all things,
> and while remaining in herself, she renews all things. . . .
> Against [Sophia] evil does not prevail. (Wis 7:22–27, 30)

Significantly for Christians, Sophia is also described as savior:

> People . . . were saved by [Sophia]. (Wis 9:18)

> A holy people and blameless race
> [Sophia] delivered from a nation of oppressors.

> She entered the soul of a servant of the Lord,
> and withstood dread kings with wonders and signs.
> She gave to holy people the reward of their labors;
> she guided them along a marvelous way,
> and became a shelter to them by day,
> and a starry flame through the night.
> She brought them over the Red Sea,
> and led them through deep waters;
> but she drowned their enemies,
> and cast them up from the depth of the sea. (Wis 10:15–19)

There are obvious connections between the Jewish figure of Sophia and the Christian understanding of the Holy Spirit. Both proceed from God and manifest an aspect of God's being in the world, and yet neither is a separate divinity; monotheism remains the container for this plurality of manifestations of the Divine.

What is highly significant is that this particular manifestation is feminine. As theologian Irene Brennan puts it, "Here we find an irrepressible desire to attribute 'feminine' characteristics to God."[8] Sophia's presence in Judaism (and the traces of her that remain in the Christian Scriptures, as in Matt 11:19 or 1 Cor 1:24) does not mean that wisdom is an attribute found only in women; it *does* illustrate the capacity of feminine images to reveal the Divine. Indeed, it has been argued that where masculine images for God are the norm, as in Judaism and Christianity, the feminine face will inevitable break through somewhere, in some form. There is a basic human need to find the feminine within the Divine.[9]

When that feminine dimension or aspect is personified, as in the Sophia literature, we are invited beyond abstract thought and into relationship. For me this has opened the door to a new avenue of prayer. Sophia is a name for God, a female name, which I can call on. She needs feminine pronouns when I speak of her. She allows the feminine face of God to take form with a concrete name, so that she is not just a motherly God, or (more abstractly still) a Father God who can be motherly. She is Sophia.

"O Wisdom . . . you reign over all things . . . : come and teach us how to live," reads a traditional Advent prayer. How different it sounded to me when I first dared to pray it to Sophia!

El Shaddai, Shekinah, Ruach: Feminine Words for God

The Hebrew language, like Greek, Latin, French, and many other ancient and modern languages, contains gendered nouns. Unlike the English language, every noun in Hebrew is either masculine or feminine. Among the vocabulary for God in the Jewish tradition are three words significant for their gender: The words translated as "the Almighty," "the presence of God," and "spirit" are all feminine. This is not merely a grammatical quirk, for these words are further pointers to a feminine dimension in imagery for the Divine.

El Shaddai or "the Almighty" can be translated as "many-breasted one," referring back to the prehistoric goddess image of the Divine as the one who nurtures her suckling children. Indeed, in Gen 49:25 the name *Shaddai* and the word for breasts (*shaddim*) occur in the same verse: "The Almighty [*Shaddai*] . . . will bless you with . . . blessings of the breasts [*shaddim*] and of the womb."[10] But this image is lost from sight in translation as "the Almighty." Indeed, it is hard to imagine two more contrasting images—the nursing mother and the impersonal all-powerful force.

Shekinah, "the presence of God," like *Sophia* became personified in Judaism, especially in its mystical form. Shekinah was the immanent (close, indwelling) aspect of the Divine—God with us, protecting us, illuminating us. In the Kabbalah, the medieval writings of the Jewish mystics, Shekinah is the divine Mother, Bride, Beloved, Daughter, Sister; she is the Cosmic Womb, the Palace, the Enclosure, the Fountain, the Garden; she is the Radiance, Word, or Glory of the unknowable Godhead who acts as friend and guide to humanity. Although the word *Shekinah* is not found in the Bible, it was used in Judaism as a name for God and is echoed in John's gospel, where God's glory is described as dwelling among us (John 1:14).

Ruach, translated as "spirit," "wind," or "breath" of God, is likewise clearly a feminine image of depth and subtlety. It is Ruach who broods over the watery chaos at creation like a mother bird, and who descends on Jesus at his baptism in the form of a dove. The early Syrian church named the Spirit "Mother" and invoked her compassionate blessings at baptisms. She is the mysterious, uncontainable breath of God who blows where she wills and brings a second birth (John 3:8). The spirit shares in the labor pangs of creation, groaning and sighing with us for freedom (Rom 8:19–26). But once again, she is lost in translation. The word for "spirit" in Greek texts is *pneuma*, a neuter word; in Latin it is the masculine *spiritus*; and English translations render "spirit" uncompromisingly male by attaching the masculine pronouns "he," "him," and "his."

Discussing theological vocabulary is more than an exercise in semantics. Language creates imagery, which in turn shapes the human imagination. It can reflect the mindset of the day, or it can break it open and point to new ways of thinking and being. Translation involves the intentional controlling of the power of language. When feminine references to God in the Bible are neutered or masculinized, a valuable lens from human experience is lost; at times a voice has been deliberately gagged. Theology, the process of speaking about God, is political, and the feminine face of God in the Bible is a contentious issue that evokes strong reactions. It is one thing to say that God is beyond gender, but it is another to use overtly feminine images and pronouns for God, even though Jesus and the Hebrew authors did just that. Historically those who developed a theology of the motherhood of God were often condemned as heretical.[11] It is no wonder that those attempting to widen the images and language for God today to include the feminine dimension do so with a degree of trepidation.

The Motherly God in the Early Church

Motherhood is only one attribute among many for the feminine, but it appears naturally and consistently not only in the Bible but also in the writings of early Christianity as a metaphor for God. Some of these writings drew on biblical feminine imagery. Others were regarded as heretical for their departure from Scripture and the emerging creeds of the church. All, however, used feminine language to convey the deep truths they perceived about the Divine.

A prominent theologian in the early church, Clement of Alexandria (ca. 150–215 CE) used striking breast-feeding imagery to describe our need of God's love:

> The Word is everything to the child, both father and mother, teacher and nurse. . . . The nutrient is the milk of the Father . . . and the Word alone supplies us children with the milk of love, and only those who suck at this breast are truly happy. . . . For this reason seeking is called sucking; to those infants who seek the Word, the Father's loving breasts supply milk.[12]

Elsewhere, he wrote that divine love transforms God the Father into a woman: "God is love, and for love of us has become woman. The ineffable being of the Father has out of compassion with us become mother. By loving, the Father has become woman."[13] Ephrem of Syria, a fourth-century theologian, drew a parallel between Eve and a feminine Holy Spirit, noting that neither is to be seen as a secondary, derivative figure: "It is not said of Eve that she was Adam's sister or his daughter, but that she came from him; likewise it is not to be said that the Spirit is a daughter or sister, but that she is from God and con-substantial with Him."[14] Contemporary with Ephrem, the author of the Macarian Homilies, wrote of a trinity of Father, Mother, and Brother, and lamented that after sin entered the world "[humanity] did not look on the true, heavenly Father, nor the good, kind Mother, the grace of the Spirit, nor the sweet, longed for Brother, the Lord" (Homily 28, 4).[15]

Originating from an unknown Judeo-Christian first- or second-century source, probably from Syria or Palestine, the *Odes of Solomon*, like Clement of Alexandria, used the image of the breast-feeding Father God, with a feminine Holy Spirit giving this divine milk to Mary, enabling her to conceive Jesus:

> A cup of milk was offered to me;
> and I drank it in the sweetness of the Lord's kindness.
> The Son is the cup,

and the Father is He who was milked;
and the Holy Spirit is She who milked Him;
because His breasts were full.

The Holy Spirit opened Her bosom,
and mixed the milk of the two breasts of the Father.
Then She gave the mixture to the generation.

The womb of the Virgin took it,
and she received conception and gave birth.
So the Virgin became a mother with great mercies.[16]

Gnostic texts are also rich with imagery of the feminine Divine. Gnostic Christianity flourished from the second century for several hundred years. Eventually condemned as heretical by those Christians who defined orthodoxy (a political as well as theological process), many of their writings nevertheless use distinctively Christian language and draw on recognizably Jewish sources. In a text on creation, for instance, the creator of the world is identified as Sophia, with her daughter Zoe (Life), also known as Eve, coming to Adam to give him life:

After the day of rest, Sophia sent Zoe, her daughter, who is called Eve, as an instructor to raise up Adam. . . . When Eve saw Adam cast down, she pitied him and said, "Adam, live! Rise up upon the earth!" Immediately her word became a deed. For when Adam rose up, immediately he opened his eyes. When he saw her, he said, "You will be called the mother of the living, because you are the one who gave me life."[17]

Gnostics depicted the Divine Mother sometimes as part of a divine couple, so that Valentinus, for example, a second-century Gnostic, refers to "the Primal Father, the Depth, the Ineffable" and "the Mother of All, Grace, Silence and the Womb." She is also identified as the Holy Spirit, in a trinity of Father, Mother, and Son. As such she is called "the image of the invisible, virginal, perfect spirit," "the mother of everything," "the matropater" (mother-father), and "the mother of many." And she is named as Wisdom, Sophia, the primal creator, teacher, and bringer of enlightenment.

Medieval Devotion to the Motherhood of God

While no Christian creed used maternal or other feminine imagery for God, and many of the (aptly named) church fathers laid out deeply sexist theology,[18] in the medieval centuries of Christianity a profound devotion to God or Christ as mother can be seen in the writings of both theologians and mystics.

St. Anselm was bishop of Canterbury in the eleventh century. A significant theologian, spiritual director, and monk, his spiritual legacy includes a long prayer to Paul in which he appeals first to Paul and then to Jesus as mothers:

> O St. Paul . . . sweet nurse, sweet mother . . . you are our greatest mother. . . . And you, Jesus, are you not also a mother? Are you not the mother who, like a hen, gathers her chickens under her wings? Truly Lord, you are a mother. . . . You, Lord God, are the great mother.[19]

In the fourteenth century, Catherine of Siena used the language of mother and nursing child to describe her experience of Jesus' playful intimacy with her:

> He behaved like a mother with her favourite child. She will show it the breast, but hold it away from it until it cries; as soon as it begins to cry, she will laugh for a while and clasp it to her and covering it with kisses, delightedly give it her full breast. So the Lord behaved with me.[20]

Two centuries later, St. Teresa of Avila (1515–1582) used similar images of breast-feeding to describe God's intimacy with and nurturing of the soul:

> The soul is like a little babe at the breast of its mother . . . receiving a divine favour.[21]

St. John of the Cross, a mystic of the same period, employs the analogy of a mother carrying a kicking child who would rather walk when he writes of our resistance to God's help:

> There are souls who, instead of committing themselves to God and making use of His help, rather hinder God by the indiscretion of their actions or by their resistance; like children who, when their mothers desire to carry them in their arms, kick and cry, insisting upon being allowed to walk, with the result that they can make no progress; and, if they advance at all, it is only at the pace of a child.[22]

Julian of Norwich (1342–ca. 1415)

By far the most profound contribution to a medieval theology of the motherhood of God comes from an English woman who lived her life as a hermit but left a remarkable text of what she called God's *Showings* or *Revelations of Divine Love*. Julian went beyond the devotional language of metaphor and analogy, such as Anselm and Teresa of Avila used, and developed a full Trinitarian theology of divine motherhood.

Julian was dangerously ill when she experienced a series of visions from God. She came to understand them as revelations of God's profound and tender love for all creation, and, having pondered their meaning for some twenty years, toward the end of her life she wrote a full account of them. Throughout this account, she explores the image of motherhood as a vehicle for describing divine love. She does this not, in the words of one of her modern commentators, as "a mere sentimental poesy as if it were only a maudlin panegyric to the 'feelings of a mother.'"[23] This is the deliberate theological language of revelation, based on a long period of sober and prayerful reflection by a woman who has been described as "a sane and conservative mystic," not someone "lost in subjectivism and peculiarity of belief."[24]

For Julian, it is absolutely necessary to use the image of motherhood if she is to convey what was revealed to her about the nature of God and of God's love. The traditional models of divine fatherhood and judgment are inadequate (even destructive) containers for her understanding of God, and so she gently but firmly redefines them with a radically new, feminine model.

Julian's starting point for her entire theology is an unshakable conviction and celebration of God's love. Everything else follows from the premise that God's love is infinite, all-inclusive, inexhaustible:

> I saw that He is to us everything which is good and comforting for our help. He is our clothing, who wraps and enfolds us for love, embraces us and shelters us, surrounds us for His love, which is so tender that He may never desert us. . . .
> There is no created being who can know how much and how sweetly and how tenderly the Creator loves us.[25]

She describes God as "familiar" and "courteous," with the properties of mercy and grace, which she sees as compassionate maternal properties. She therefore balances the traditional doctrine of the fatherhood of God with her understanding of divine motherhood, affirming that "God rejoices that He is our Father, and God rejoices that He is our Mother" (ch. 52).

Julian extends divine motherhood also to Jesus, developing the image vividly by referring to pregnancy and labor, as "He carries us within Him in love and travail" (ch. 60). She goes on to say that "our precious Mother Jesus can feed us with Himself, and does, most courteously and tenderly, with the blessed sacrament" (ch. 60).

So fundamental is Julian's doctrine of divine motherly love that it underpins her teaching on sin and forgiveness. Countering centuries-old and biblically-based doctrines of the wrath of God, divine judgment, and eternal hellfire for the damned, Julian writes that God can never be angry, because "His power, His wisdom, His charity and His unity do not allow Him to be angry" (ch. 46). And in words reminiscent of the biblical passages considered earlier, in which

God's intimate bond with humankind is likened to the bond between mother and child, Julian states:

> Between God and our souls there is neither wrath nor forgiveness in His sight. For our soul is so wholly united to God, through His own goodness, that between God and our soul nothing can interpose. (46)

Her faith in God's unconditional love leads Julian to declare:

> All will be well, and all will be well, and every kind of thing will be well. (27)

Julian recognizes that this clashes with the church's teaching on eternal damnation, but she has seen a deeper truth. She writes that when she questioned God about this, God reassured her by saying that what seems impossible to her is not a divine impossibility, and that "I shall make everything well" (ch. 32). And so, Julian concludes, it is good for us

> hastily to flee from everything that is not good, and to fall into our Lord's breast, as a child into the mother's arms, with all our intention and with all our mind, knowing our feebleness and our great need, knowing His everlasting goodness and His blessed love, seeking only in Him for salvation, cleaving to Him with faithful trust. (74)

Many years ago, as a child, I visited Norwich while on holiday. If I were to go back now, it would be as a pilgrim to Mother Julian's cell. In the seas of controversy over appropriate language for God, Julian's writings are like solid rock under my feet. She had no political agenda; she simply stated with unshakeable faith that God's mother-love can be depended upon without exception. Her words read, prayed, and meditated upon have the power to erase the dark images of divine wrath that alienate and terrify. Julian was an unself-conscious pioneer in theological territory, and I treasure the legacy she left.

The medieval mystics who employed the metaphor of motherhood to convey their teachings about God have been called "proto-feminists" for breaking with the traditional theology of their day, which stressed God's absolute transcendence and patriarchal will, and replacing it with an emphasis on God's maternal intimacy and unconditional love.[26] They did not do this, however, to elevate the role of motherhood in society, to better the position of women, or to challenge patriarchy in the church. Rather, they were led to these maternal images by the desire to give words to their mystical experiences of union with God.

All religious language is ultimately metaphorical. To describe God and the divine-human relationship, we need a rich, varied, and complex language. Of course, in the end, such language is still only a pointer to God, not a container. Every theological statement we make deserves at least a mental "as it were" appended to it: God is love (as it were); God is like a mother (as it were); Jesus is Lord (as it were).

The contemplatives of the mystical tradition used metaphors freely, creatively, and unconventionally because they *knew*, they did not merely believe in an abstract, academic way, that the God they had experienced was radically beyond any human attempts at a precise definition. Metaphor, like poetry, does not define but reveals. It is truthful without being literal.

Maternal imagery for God is not "just a metaphor"; rather, it is metaphorical language that conveys a deep truth about God's being. To describe God with maternal attributes is a radical departure from the norm of patriarchal, male-identified language, but it is not merely a feminist gesture; it is an attempt to use the best metaphors available to talk about certain aspects of the Divine. If we do not use images from female experience, we impoverish and restrict our ability to imagine God.

Mother Mary as the Feminine Face of God

The last component of my research concerned Mariology, the doctrine of Mary the mother of Jesus. As an Anglican, I saw Mary as part of the Christian story (largely in its nativity and crucifixion scenes) but had not developed a devotion to her. I was aware that in Roman Catholicism she played a central role; Catholic acquaintances of mine would pray to Mary rather than God, to my disapproving Protestant mind. Yet Mary is a highly ambivalent religious figure. She is seen on the one hand as the epitome of female submission and receptivity to the divine (masculine) will, humbly bowing her head and saying Yes to what is going to be done to her; and on the other hand as a symbol of female power and autonomy, crowned as Queen of Heaven and honored as Mother of God. "Whose side is Mary on?" asks feminist theologian Rosemary Radford Ruether.[27] In a sense, the Mary of the Gospels is no more than a vessel into which has been poured a variety of contents, from Mary as "the good girl of Christianity," as feminist scholar Naomi Goldenberg puts it, "the only pin-up girl who has been permitted in monks' cells throughout the ages,"[28] to Mary as goddess, the deified feminine, or the womanly face of God. As I studied Mariology I saw Mary's evolution in religious thought from peasant mother to divine queen.

Mary as we meet her in the Bible is decidedly human. She miraculously conceives a child without a father, but this is God's miracle, not her own. She has a husband and other children. She worries, wonders, asks questions. She is frustrated by her growing son; she fears for his sanity when he is the adult Jesus, an itinerant preacher and healer; she stands helplessly by at his crucifixion; and she vanishes from the record after his resurrection.

But in the Christian imagination Mary was the sinless woman, the second Eve, the perfect mother to a sinless Christ who was the second Adam. As her son was acclaimed Son of God and, ultimately, God the Son, so Mary was hailed as his divinized counterpart. Paralleling his virginal conception, Mary herself was believed to have been immaculately conceived, that is, conceived without parental sexual activity, and therefore free from the sexually transmitted stain of original sin. Mary's virginity became a perpetual attribute (and her other children were therefore seen as stepchildren or nieces and nephews), so that she was the sinless and humanly anomalous virgin-mother.

In a similar parallel, after Jesus was declared by the Council of Nicea in 321 to be "God of God," "of one substance with the Father," the Council of Ephesus in 431 proclaimed Mary to be *Theotokos*, "Mother of God." And by that time she had also been portrayed from biblical images as the Bride of Christ (Eph 5:27), Wisdom-Sophia, and the heavenly woman clothed with the sun and standing on the moon (Rev 12:1).

The final development was made Roman Catholic dogma in 1950, when Mary's bodily assumption into heaven was declared infallible truth. Mirroring Jesus' ascension into heaven (Luke 24:51; Acts 1:9), this dogma proclaimed that Mary did not die but fell asleep and was carried up to heaven to be enthroned with her Son, uncorrupted by death. Together with the doctrines of Mary's immaculate conception, perpetual virginity, and sinlessness, the doctrine of her assumption into heaven effectively eradicated her humanity and deified her.

But Christianity did not develop in a cultural vacuum. Apart from its Jewish roots it also grew up in a context where the worship of goddesses was the norm and had been practiced for thousands of years. The Mediterranean cradle of Christianity was home to the cults of Greek goddesses such as Athena, the goddess of wisdom, and Demeter, the Great Mother; Canaanite goddesses such as Ashtaroth, the goddess of heaven; and Egyptian goddesses such as Isis, the goddess of the elements. Both deliberately and unconsciously, Mary became associated with these goddesses, acquiring their titles, functions, and festivals. As Ruether writes, Mary as mother goddess in popular devotion

> is venerated for her helping power in natural crises. She helps the women through birth-pangs, the farmer's cow through delivery. Like the goddesses of old, she assures the coming of the new rains, the new grain, the new lamb. She is the maternal image of the divine who understands the daily needs of ordinary people and who renews the processes of nature upon which they depend for life.[29]

Commenting on the declaration of Mary as *Theotokos* in Ephesus, Ruether writes, "It is not accidental that the declaration . . . took place amid scenes of fanatical enthusiasm by the populace of a city that had once given its enthusiastic support to another virgin mother, the great Artemis of Ephesus (see Acts 19)."[30]

In religious art the connections between Mary and the pre-Christian goddesses become vividly evident, as Mary was literally robed with their garments and placed on their thrones. One of the clearest examples comes from a comparison of Egyptian religious art depicting Isis, the mother of the gods Horus and Osiris, with Christian art portraying Mary with Jesus. For those more familiar with Christian art, it comes as a shock to see images of the Egyptian goddess nursing her son Horus at her breast, like a Madonna and Child, and cradling the dead body of her adult son Osiris across her knees, as Michelangelo depicted Mary with the dead Christ in his Pietà sculpture. We are used to seeing the Christian culture as normative; it requires a shift in consciousness to recognize that much of it was derived from earlier peoples and their religions.

Enthroned in heaven, yet retaining her qualities as compassionate mother, Mary became the gentle face of God—the warm, emotional savior. This development was in direct relation to the hardening of the images of Jesus and the Father in Christendom, as they were presented more and more as heavenly rulers—remote, judgmental, and imperious. Feminist theologian Elisabeth Schüssler Fiorenza has named this "the patriarchalization of the God image," and comments that, in reaction to this, "Mary became the 'other face,' the Christian 'face' of God."[31]

In his study of Mary, Geoffrey Ashe explains: "The universe is split at the summit. God stands for Justice, and since we are all sinners more or less, most of us have little to hope for at his hands. Mary stands for Mercy, and it is only because of her influence at court, not because of love or goodwill on God's part, that heaven is within reach for more than a handful of human beings."[32] Ashe offers numerous examples of prayers to Mary, from the fifth century on, where she is clearly addressed as merciful savior, in contrast to God the Judge. In 717, for instance, when Constantinople had been saved from the army of Leo the Isaurian, patriarch Germanus held a festival in Mary's honor to thank her for delivering the city by her prayers. In his sermon were the following words:

> No one, Lady all holy, is saved except through you. . . . You, having maternal power with God, can obtain abundant forgiveness for even the greatest sinners. For . . . God obeys you through and in all things, as his true mother. . . . You turn away the just threat and the sentence of damnation, because you love the Christians. . . . Therefore the Christian people trustfully turn to you, refuge of sinners.[33]

Indeed, as Marian devotion continued and flourished into the medieval period, legends were told of Mary capriciously helping complete rogues, no matter how undeserving, if they loved her. Mary alone could approach the heavenly throne without fear and trembling. She could break the rules. She could put in a good word for the sinner, so that God's wrath might be turned aside.

The following extract from a fourteenth century Franciscan book shows how this polarity between the gentle mother and harsh father was played out in Christian devotions: "When we have offended Christ, we should first go to the Queen of heaven and offer her . . . prayers, fasting, vigils and alms; then she, like a mother, will come between thee and Christ, the father who wishes to beat us, and she will throw the cloak of her mercy between the rod of punishment and us, and soften the king's anger against us."[34] Six centuries later, in the present day, Mary is still viewed essentially the same way. She is, for many Christians, the softer, gentler savior. As authors Ronda Chervin and Mary Neill write: "[Mary is] the divinized face and heart we seek. She is the mother of joy, compassion, endurance. . . . Suffering and joy find in her a steady centre. . . . She is ever the compassionate one who, when there is a clash between love and law, makes sure that love always wins."[35] One is reminded of the "Princess Diana effect." As Diana became more beloved, adulated, and idolized as "the people's princess," so the House of Windsor was increasingly perceived as stiff, remote, and unfeeling. Paradoxically, then, devotion to Mary as compassionate savior can therefore further alienate worshipers from an already distant God. If the feminine is equated with the soft and loving, and if that in turn is equated with the characteristics of Mary, the Godhead remains by implication masculine, hard, and judgmental.

As Marina Warner concludes her substantial study of Mary, she reflects on the dynamic of devotion to Mary, which has raised her to the status of goddess or at least co-redemptrix:

> A goddess is better than no goddess at all, for the sombre-suited masculine world of the Protestant religion is altogether too much like a gentlemen's club to which the ladies are only admitted on special days. . . . [Yet] it should not be necessary to have a goddess contrasted with a god, a divinity who stands for qualities considered the quintessence of femininity and who thus polarizes symbolic and religious thought into two irreconcilably opposed camps.[36]

Psychologist Carl Jung, in whose lifetime the doctrine of Mary's assumption into heaven was proclaimed, saw this not as a recognition of her divinity but as a recognition of the feminine aspect of the Divine. He considered that a "quaternity" of Father, Son, Holy Spirit, and Mary was a more complete and balanced picture of the Godhead than a (masculine) Trinity. And he argued that the feminine within God, like the masculine, demands an equally personal representation.

Others have interpreted Mary's role in Christianity along similar lines, focusing not on Mary herself but on Mary as a symbol of certain divine attributes. So A. M. Greeley, for example, in *The Mary Myth*, writes: "Mary is a symbol of the feminine component of the deity. She represents the human insight that the Ultimate is passionately tender, seductively attractive, irresistibly inspiring, and graciously healing."[37] Linking Mary with pre-Christian feminine images for the divine, Greeley evocatively summarizes the process of Mary's development in religious thought: "All the old goddesses came creeping out of their caves, went through an extraordinary rehabilitation, and emerged in the person of Mary, the mother of Jesus.[38] Like the Buddhist who sees the Buddha as a finger pointing to the moon, Greeley sees Mary pointing to certain attributes within God. Thus, Mary reveals God to us as passionately loving, life giving, tender, hope inspiring, gentle, generous, full of grace, renewing, transforming, alluring, all-embracing. As the subtitle of his book makes clear, Mary is a myth (that is, a religious truth conveyed in a nonliteral way) that reveals the femininity of God.

Conclusions and Questions

From Mother Mary to Mother God, from Sophia to Spirit, a rich vein of feminine imagery for the Divine runs through the Bible and Christian spirituality. As I stumbled upon it, brought it to the surface, and sifted through it, I felt a mixture of emotions: vindication, that this layer did exist, hidden deep below the surface that had become the norm; sadness, that I had never been taught it, never known it; anticipation, as I began to see the ramifications of an emergent feminist theology; but perhaps most fundamentally of all, I felt recognition of a God who could look like me.

Until that time, God had been he, and I am she. I loved God and believed that God loved me and had called me to ministry in the church. But all around were voices saying No, I must have made a mistake, God could not have called me to be a priest because I am a woman. There was something about being a woman that disabled me, made me lose my footing, doubt myself, while God-as-he looked favorably on male priests, theologians, ordinands. Teresa of Avila is said to have lamented, "The very thought that I am a woman is enough to make my wings droop." Her words mirrored my sense of hesitancy, defeat, inadequacy.

But when God is she, there is more than a shift in vocabulary; the very air that we breathe is changed. I recognize something of myself in God, and I see something of God in me. The hesitancy lifts; I no longer need to justify my vocation or apologize for my difference. There is a new norm, a new starting point, the possibility of a new heaven and a new earth.

My essay completed, I hugged these new insights to me as a source of strength. I did not nail them to the door of the college chapel and take my stand beside them. I did not even discuss them, except in casual "Did you know?" conversations with David. I had mapped the way in which there has consistently been an instinctive human reaching for the feminine in speaking of God, but just as instinctively I knew that the map was dangerous. If I followed its paths, where would it lead?

Several years later I read Ruether's words about the insufficiency of a feminine dimension for the Divine: "We need to go beyond the idea of a 'feminine side' of God, whether to be identified with the Spirit or even with the Sophia-Spirit together, and question the assumption that the highest symbol of divine sovereignty still remains exclusively male."[39] It may also be noted that a motherly God can easily become a smothering God who fosters dependence in perpetually childlike worshipers, while a simplistic equation of femininity with nurturance and compassion is as sexist as the assumption that all males are domineering and harsh.

Motherhood and apple pie theology is eventually unsatisfying. Its sweetness becomes saccharine, and women are once again in the kitchen as wives and mothers, offering a feminine dimension of God as an optional extra. A more robust, thoroughgoing theology is necessary, where the dominant voice is not masculine and the cultural norms are turned upside down. "God needs to be liberated from our theology," writes Eleanor McLaughlin. "Theology is not a tabernacle to contain the One who is Ahead, but it is a sign on the way, and thus is provisional. Thus the theologian is not only protester and prophet, if she is lucky, but also pilgrim."[40]

In the two decades since I wrote my paper on the motherhood of God, I have been a pilgrim. The journey began with the uncovering of a forgotten face, but it could not end there. I was led, sometimes pushed, to go deeper and further beyond automatic assumptions and easy clichés. Several times along the way I have been afraid that my faith has disintegrated. Often I have worried that the journey will change me so much that my marriage will break apart, or I will have to leave (or be ejected from) the Christian church. But I can no more stop the pilgrimage than I could stop the frightening, disorientating labor pains when my children were being born. Now I recognize the pains and fears when they come, and I am learning to breathe through them, with my chosen midwives close at hand.

One place along the pilgrimage has been the home of the Goddess—the cultures, peoples, and religions that did not know Yahweh or Jesus but worshiped female deities. Cautiously, fearing for my orthodoxy in the presence of pure paganism, I ventured into a very different world.

Notes

1. Mary Daly, *Beyond God the Father* (Boston: Beacon, 1973), 184.

2. Elisabeth Moltmann-Wendel and Jürgen Moltmann, "Becoming Human in New Community," in *The Community of Men and Women in the Church* (ed. Constance Parvey; Geneva: World Council of Churches, 1983), 29.

3. See, e.g., Monica Sjoo and Barbara Mor, *The Great Cosmic Mother: Rediscovering the Religion of the Earth* (San Francisco: HarperSanFrancisco, 1987), 55–56, 63.

4. Augustine of Hippo (354–430 CE.) wrote: "The woman, together with her own husband, is the image of God, so that the whole substance may be one image. But when she is referred to separately in her quality as a helpmeet, which regards the woman alone, then she is not the image of God. But, as regards the man alone, he is the image of God as fully and completely as when the woman too is joined with him in one" (*De Trinitate* 7.7, 10).

5. On the word *Elohim* as plural and feminine, see James S. Forrester-Brown, *The Two Creation Stories in Genesis* (Berkeley, Calif.: Shambala, 1974), 17.

6. For a discussion of the womblike compassion of God, see Marcus Borg, *Meeting Jesus Again for the First Time* (San Francisco: HarperSanFrancisco, 1994), 47–49.

7. Wisdom literature is found in both the Old Testament and in the Apocrypha. The Apocrypha is a collection of books received by the early church as part of the Greek version of the Old Testament but that are not included in the Hebrew Bible. Some or all of these books are regarded as canonical by the Roman Catholic and Eastern Orthodox Churches, respectively, but not by most Protestant groups.

8. Irene Brennan, "Women in the Kingdom of God," *The Month*, 2nd ser., 13, no. 12 (December 1980): 414–17.

9. In his study of Mary the mother of Jesus, Geoffrey Ashe writes that the feminine personification of wisdom emerged in Judaism because "Israel's God had become too remote in his heaven beyond the sky." Ashe, *The Virgin* (London: Routledge and Kegan Paul, 1976), 28.

10. I am grateful to my friend and Old Testament scholar Paul Joyce for this reference.

11. See Elaine Pagels, *The Gnostic Gospels* (Middlesex, England: Weidenfeld and Nicolson, 1980), 17.

12. Quoted in Elaine Pagels, "What Became of God the Mother?" in *Womanspirit Rising* (ed. Carol P. Christ and Judith Plaskow; San Francisco: Harper Collins, 1992), 116–17.

13. Quoted in Woman's Guild/Panel on Doctrine, Church of Scotland, *The Motherhood of God* (ed. Alan E. Lewis; Edinburgh: St. Andrew Press, 1984), 49–50.

14. Quoted by R. Murray in his study of early Syriac Christianity, *Symbols of Church and Kingdom* (Cambridge: Cambridge University Press, 1975), 318.

15. Quoted in R. Murray, *Symbols of Church and Kingdom* (Cambridge: Cambridge University Press, 1975), 318.

16. James Charlesworth, trans., *The Odes of Solomon* (Oxford: Clarendon Press, 1973), Ode 19, 1–7.

17. James M. Robinson, ed., *Nag Hammadi Library* (San Francisco: Harper and Row, 1977), 172

18. Tertullian (ca. 160–225 CE), for example, described women as "the devil's gateway," and saw women as the cause of sin, on account of whom Christ had to die. His contemporary Origen claimed that "God does not stoop to look upon what is feminine and of the flesh."

19. St. Anselm, *Prayers and Meditations* (trans. Benedicta Ward; London: Penguin Books, 1973), 152–56.

20. Quoted in G. Lamb, *The Life of St. Catherine of Siena* (London: Harvill Press, 1960), 175.

21. St. Teresa of Avila, *The Way of Perfection* (London: T. Baker, 1935), ch. 31, 7.

22. St. John of the Cross, *Ascent of Mount Carmel* (trans. E. Allison Peers; London: Burns, Oates and Washbourne, 1934), Prologue 3.

23. Julian of Norwich, *Showings* (trans. Edmund Colledge and James Walsh; New York: Paulist Press, 1978), 10.

24. R. H. Thouless, *The Lady Julian* (London: SPCK, 1924), 94–95.

25. Julian of Norwich, *Showings*, chs. 5, 6.

26. Elizabeth Clark and Herbert Richardson, ed., *Women and Religion: The Original Sourcebook of Women in Christian Thought* (San Francisco: Harper and Row, 1977), 102.

27. Rosemary Radford Ruether, *New Woman/New Earth* (New York: Seabury, 1975), 37.

28. Naomi Goldenberg, *Changing of the Gods* (Boston: Beacon, 1979), 75.

29. Rosemary Radford Ruether, *Mary, the Feminine Face of the Church* (London: SCM Press, 1979), 47.

30. Ibid., 49.

31. Elisabeth Schüssler Fiorenza, "Feminist Spirituality, Christian Identity, and Catholic Vision," in *Womanspirit Rising* (ed. Carol P. Christ and Judith Plaskow; San Francisco: Harper Collins, 1992), 138.

32. Ashe, *Virgin*, 203.

33. Quoted in Ashe, *Virgin*, 202–3.

34. Quoted in Marina Warner, *Alone of All Her Sex* (London: Weidenfeld and Nicolson, 1976), 285.

35. Ronda Chervin and Mary Neill, *Bringing the Mother with You* (New York: Seabury, 1982), 6.

36. Warner, *Alone of All Her Sex*, 338.

37. A. M. Greeley, *The Mary Myth: On the Femininity of God* (New York: Seabury, 1977), 13.

38. Ibid., 80.

39. Rosemary Radford Ruether, *Sexism and God-Talk* (London: SCM Press, 1983), 61.

40. Joan Arnold Romero, "The Protestant Principle" in *Religion and Sexism* (ed. Rosemary Radford Ruether; New York: Simon and Schuster, 1974), 339.

CHAPTER 2
Searching for the Goddess

Remembering Her

"AT THE VERY DAWN OF RELIGION, God was a woman. Do you remember?" These haunting words come near the beginning of feminist historian Merlin Stone's study of ancient Goddess-worshiping religions.[1] She and others have documented from archaeology how the Divine as Goddess was venerated for some 25,000 years in prehistoric and early historic times. The male God of Judaism, Christianity, and Islam, by comparison, has been on the religious scene for a mere 4,000 years.

But did I remember? No. I knew nothing about this Goddess or her religion. I was aware that the classical Romans and Greeks had worshiped goddesses and gods in their pantheon of deities, and I knew that contemporary Eastern religions continued this practice, with hundreds of male and female deities, all with names that were foreign and meaningless to me. But this was polytheism, and I had been taught to regard it as spiritually inferior to monotheism and culturally more primitive. These gods and goddesses seemed laughably human (and therefore invented) with their foibles, petty rivalries, sexual couplings, and erratic interfering with human affairs.

A sole, prehistoric Great Mother Goddess seemed more primitive still—an Earth Mother worshiped in ignorance and superstition by a people who lived in total dependence on the land, with its terrifying, incomprehensible powers. How could she possibly have anything to do with me? Yet as archaeological studies in the latter part of this century have shown, this Goddess was venerated by peoples from the Paleolithic period of 25,000 BCE, through the Neolithic, Bronze, and Iron Ages, and up to ca. 500 CE.[2] The cultures in which she was the symbol of divinity became highly developed and urbanized, forcing historians, as the evidence emerged, to rewrite their accounts of the birth of civilization. Through places that we now know as Crete, Turkey, France, Greece, Egypt, Palestine, Lebanon, Spain, Russia, Iraq, Italy, Israel, Jordan, Ethiopia, Cyprus, and beyond, the Goddess was worshiped as creator, lawmaker, inventor of language and the alphabet, healer, giver of wisdom, valiant leader, mother of all, source of intelligence, and bringer of order, rhythm, and truth to the world.

The patronizing or misguided view that Goddess worship was merely a primitive fertility cult of unsophisticated peoples has been rightly criticized by Stone as "a gross over-simplification of a complex theological structure."[3] She points out that, far from being merely an Earth Mother (and inferior to a Sky God such as Yahweh), she was venerated in the Near and Middle East as Queen of Heaven, and by the Inuit, Japanese, Khasis of India, Canaanites, Australians, Anatolians, and Arabians as a Sun Goddess.

With many different titles, functions, and names, she was yet one concept—Goddess, a universal deity, "much as people today think of God."[4] Whether called Sarasvati in India, Brigit in Ireland, Demeter in Greece, Isis in Egypt, Ishtar in Mesopotamia, Astarte in Canaan, Aphrodite in Cyprus, or Inanna in Sumeria, she was one, and from her came all that was. Motherhood was a natural attribute for her, and she was depicted as a pregnant woman, large-breasted and sometimes in the act of giving birth. The so-called "Venus figurines," Paleolithic and Neolithic sculptures of female forms, found in their thousands throughout Europe, are not prehistoric *Playboy* models for the erotic amusement of males, as was once thought, but are ancient symbols of the Goddess and her powers of creativity and regeneration.

Other symbols associated with the Goddess were similarly taken from the world of nature. She was represented by serpents, butterflies, water, does, eggs, fish, birds, sun, and moon. More abstractly, she was symbolized by the circle, the spiral, and the labyrinth. She was associated with both birth and death, darkness and light, for she was the source and end of all. When depicted with her son or brother, lover or consort—a later development when humans understood the role of the male in conception—the Goddess remained central and supreme, for unlike the myth of Eve's creation from Adam's rib, our ancestors acknowledged that the male was brought forth from the female.

Goddess Cultures

A culture is called prehistoric if it predates the invention of writing. Yet there is much we can learn without the aid of written records, from the archaeological study of a culture's art, architecture, burial practices, religious artifacts, and myths. As literacy developed, the orally transmitted stories of ancient peoples were written down and became another source of information for historians.

In her book *The Chalice and the Blade*[5], Riane Eisler has pieced together this sort of archaeological and historical information about Goddess cultures and, building on the work of scholars such as Merlin Stone, Marija Gimbutas, and James Mellaart, has constructed a vivid picture of the worldview, social structures, and gender relations of these cultures. Focusing especially on the Minoan culture in Crete, a Goddess-worshiping civilization which flourished from ca. 6000 BCE to ca. 1400 BCE and outlasted other Neolithic Goddess cultures by some two thousand years, Eisler presents a picture of what she calls a partnership society—a society in which there were no marked distinctions in status between male and female, rich and poor, strong and weak.

What is *not* present in Neolithic and Minoan sites is as important as what is found there. There are, for example, no lavish burial sites for wealthy rulers; no remains of slaves or animals sacrificed at the death of a ruler; no military fortifications; no depictions of war; no caches of weapons; no evidence of damage through warfare over a period of 1,500 years; no evidence that women were regarded as inferior to or weaker than men. Instead, the art depicts women and men as equally prominent in leadership, cultic activities, and public life. Sexuality is portrayed as natural and unashamed, with neither gender relating to the other as sexual object or possession. Families were almost certainly matrilineal—that is, tracing the descent through the mother—but not matriarchal, with women controlling or dominating men. Symbols of the sacred are found everywhere, because, as Eisler puts it, "Religion was life, and life was religion."[6] Sacred and secular were not separated.

Living in large settlements, developing agriculture and livestock, using metallurgical skills for art and utensils rather than for weaponry, and living peaceably without need of fortifications of armies, the Neolithic culture as it flourished in Crete and elsewhere was, in Eisler's words, a partnership society where "a spirit of harmony between men and women as joyful and equal participants in life appears to pervade."[7] At its center was the figure of the Goddess, source and blessing of all, bestowing and awakening life and the love of life, not destruction and the fear of death.

There is something undeniably appealing about this image of a long vanished culture, especially for women. As I read Eisler's work and imagined what life in such a culture might have been like, I felt a deep longing for it to be true. But is it fact or fiction, history or myth? Eisler is convinced that the excavations on Crete have revealed "firm confirmation from our past that our hopes for peaceful human coexistence are not, as we are so often told, 'utopian dreams.'"[8] Others, feminists among them, have been reluctant to pin too much on this evidence, which seems too good to be true. It is as though we cannot bring ourselves to believe that this sort of culture once existed but now is lost, believing instead that it appears merely as an improbable illusion to our jaundiced eyes. So these cultural studies are dismissed as golden age myths or utopian fantasies. At best, we are told, Goddess cultures existed but failed to survive, unsuited to newer cultural developments. They are therefore unworkable anachronisms for our own day, belonging to a distant and very different past.

Yet when we consider the reasons for the decline of the Goddess cultures we find, paradoxically, further evidence for their existence, their respect for the feminine, and their radically different worldview. As warring forces moved into Old Europe (7000–5000 BCE) and the Near and Middle East, hostile to the cultures of the Goddess, it is clear that they attacked what they viewed as a threat. And they did so in the name of a new deity, whom we now know as God.

Where Did She Go? How the Goddess Vanished

Stone refutes the idea that Goddess worship gradually died out as a spiritually superior male monotheism took its place. Instead, she believes that it was the victim of a long period of deliberate suppression and persecution by the leaders of the newer religions with their male deities. She relates the history of the invasion of the settled civilizations and agricultural settlements of Old Europe by Indo-European (Kurgan) warring nomadic tribes, and explains how the aggressive invaders deliberately dismantled the female-honoring aspects of the lands they conquered in order to establish and perpetuate their control.

These invaders came from Russia and the Caucasus region, to the north and east of the Goddess cultures. Their homelands were less hospitable than the fertile areas they attacked, and they had developed only a rudimentary form of agriculture. Nomadic hunters and sheepherders, they depended upon constant movement and incursion into new lands to find pastures for their flocks. As they went, armed with iron weapons and horse-drawn chariots, they found no effective resistance to their might.

From about 4300 to 2800 BCE, waves of these invasions took place. Archaeologist Marija Gimbutas summarizes the vast differences between the invaders and the people whose lands they seized:

> The Old European belief system focused on the agricultural cycle of birth, death, and regeneration, embodied in the feminine principle, a Mother Creatrix. The Kurgan ideology . . . exalted virile, heroic warrior gods of the shining and thunderous sky. Weapons are non-existent in Old European imagery; whereas the dagger and battle-axe are dominant symbols of the Kurgans, who like all historically known Indo-Europeans, glorified the lethal power of the sharp blade.[9]

Always on the move, warring, led by warrior chiefs, the culture of the invaders was patrilinear and patriarchal, in contrast to the matrilineal, egalitarian societies they conquered. They built their settlements on hills, with fortified headquarters and semi-subterranean houses. Aggressive invasions with massive destruction and bloodshed were followed by settlement and occupancy of the new lands, with tight control exerted in order to maintain their ascendancy. Conquered peoples were enslaved, and the women taken as wives or sexual booty. Sophisticated civilizations were plunged into chaos, and a cultural twilight descended.

As two strikingly different cultural forces met and clashed, so too did their deities. The invaders worshiped a storm god, associated with mountains, fire, lightning, and light, and symbolized by the battle-axe or blade. In myths originating from this turbulent period, the male deity battled with the Goddess as Marduk fought Tiamat in Babylonian myth; Zeus fought the serpent, son and symbol of Gaia in Greece; and Yahweh struggled with Leviathan, the Canaanite sea serpent representing the Goddess Lat in the Hebrew culture. We have more recent mythic battles in the stories of St. George and the dragon (another Goddess symbol), and St. Patrick and the snakes in Ireland.

Resolution of the battle took place in different ways. For a while the male and female deities coexisted and were worshiped together, but gradually the Goddess was reduced and suppressed as myths were told in which she became the subservient wife of the male deity or was raped, killed, or masculinized. Thus, the creator goddess Tiamat was mythically murdered by Marduk, the Canaanite goddess Astarte was renamed Ashtoreth (a male name), and Athena was transformed from the goddess of wisdom to the patron of warriors. The process happened slowly but inexorably, beginning with the Kurgan invasions, continuing through the Iron Age in which the Hebrew people invaded Canaan, and being brought to completion in the Roman era, when Christianity became the imperial religion and all lingering traces of Goddess worship were suppressed.

In tandem with the removal of the Goddess from her central position in the invaded cultures, the conquerors—whether Kurgan, in the fourth century BCE, or Hebrew, in the first century BCE—consistently removed women's sexual, economic, and legal rights. They recognized that the imposition and maintenance of a dominator society, ruled by might and enforced by rigid controls, was severely undermined by a culture that embraced partnership ideals and valued the feminine. In particular, a matrilineal society was seen as a threat to patriarchal control, and so women became reduced, as the Goddess was, to be subordinate to men as wives, chattel, dependants.

In the Hebrew context, for which the Bible provides ample evidence, we see the following pattern typical of this long period of invasion:

> The invaders, under orders from Yahweh, attack Canaan, destroy its defenses, massacre whole populations, plunder its goods, and eliminate its religious practices (see, e.g., Exod 34:11–16; Deut 2:31–36; 3:3–7; 12:2–3; Josh 6:20–21; 8:18–29; 10:28–42).

> Virginal women among the conquered people are taken as booty, to become Hebrew wives (see, e.g., Num 31:17–18, 32–35; Deut 21:10–13).

Worship of any deity but Yahweh is punishable by death (see, e.g., Deut 13:6–16).

Women who are found not to be virginal before marriage, or who have sexual relations outside of marriage, are to be stoned to death (see, e.g., Deut 22:20–21).

Women are defined as the possession of their menfolk (see, e.g., Exod 20:17).

Women are said to be subordinate to men by divine ordinance (see Gen 3:16).

The giving of life through childbirth is seen as ritually defiling (see, e.g., Lev 12:2–8), while the taking of life, the exacting of brutal punishments, and the use of terrifying threats is accepted as normative and necessary (see, e.g., Lev 20:1–16; Deut 28:15–68).

Hebrew culture became hierarchical—a culture ruled by priests, as God's sacred authorities on earth. The priests' most powerful weapons were, in Eisler's words, "the 'sacred' stories, rituals, and priestly edicts through which they systematically inculcated in peoples' minds the fear of terrible, remote, and 'inscrutable' deities. For people had to be taught to obey the deities—and their earthly representatives— who now arbitrarily exercised the powers of life and death."10

The priestly school rewrote much of the Hebrew Scriptures around 400 BCE in order to reinforce its control. As part of that rewriting the priests told the myth of Adam and Eve, a contrived mythology according to anthropologist Joseph Campbell. In his *Masks of God*, he wrote that the goddess-centered myths of the civilizations conquered by the Hebrews were deliberately turned on their head and "became inverted, to render an argument just the opposite to that of its origin."11 It was a cautionary tale and myth of the origin of evil designed to deter the Hebrews from any attempt to follow the old religion of the Goddess.

Adam and Eve Revisited

From my Christian upbringing, I thought I knew what the Adam and Eve story in Gen 3 was about. It was not necessarily to be understood literally, but, like all mythology, conveyed an inner truth within an outer story. I accepted the traditional view that it was an attempt to explain the origin of evil and suffering in the world, with the serpent representing the devil who brought about humanity's fall from grace into sin. It described the essential weakness and capacity for sin that characterizes human nature, from which only Christ as the Second Adam could free us. And it accounted for our fundamental alienation from God, depicted in the expulsion of Adam and Eve from the garden of Eden.

But the myth can be read very differently if its central symbols are seen against the backdrop of the suppression of Goddess worship by the Hebrew Yahwists. Like the characters and symbols in a political cartoon, each has a specific meaning and association that is relevant to and recognized by contemporary audiences. In this light, the serpent is at once recognized as the ancient symbol of the Goddess. Although it came later to represent fertility (as a phallic symbol) or the devil, originally it represented the wisdom of the Goddess, and it is found in art and artifacts from Crete to Philistia, Egypt to Greece. In the religion of the Hebrews, however, the serpent was not the bearer of wisdom but the enemy of Yahweh.

The tree of the knowledge of good and evil, set in the middle of the garden and forbidden by Yahweh to Adam and Eve, was probably a sycamore fig tree, as Gen 3:7 suggests. This tree was considered sacred, and to eat of its fruit was to eat of the flesh of the Goddess and thus participate in her life. Its fruit was honored in the Egyptian worship of the goddess Hathor as the food of eternity, of life after death, of immortality. Its wood was used to make regal coffins, symbolizing the return of the body to the goddess for regeneration. The "asherah" condemned in the Hebrew Scriptures as idols or poles at pagan worship sites were probably sycamore fig trees.[12] What Yahweh is forbidding in this story is therefore any dealings with the religion of the Goddess.

Furthermore, this story, together with the version of the creation story in Gen 2, inverts the wisdom of the old religion by attacking or contradicting it in every detail:

The creator deity is Yahweh, not the Mother Goddess (Gen 2:4).

Adam is created first, not male and female together (Gen 2:7; cf. 1 Tim 2:13).

Adam alone is understood to be in the divine image (see 1 Cor 11:7).

Eve is created secondarily, from Adam's body (Gen 2:21–22).

Eve is given to Adam to be his helper (Gen 2:20–22; cf. 1 Cor 11:9).

Eve's temptation by the serpent, her eating of the fruit, and her giving of the fruit to Adam is seen as evidence of her gullibility, folly, and guilt—for which she bears the blame of bringing sin into the world (see 1 Tim 2:14).

The punishment for Eve is that childbirth will be much more painful and she will be ruled by and dependent upon her husband (Gen 3:16).

Adam is chastised for listening to his wife (Gen 3:17).

Both are banished from the garden (agrarian life) and kept at bay by a flaming sword (warring nomad culture) (Gen 3:23–24).

The message is clear: Goddess religion is an evil temptation which will bring about severe penalties if practiced; women (the priestesses and prophetesses of the Goddess, who were often portrayed as receiving their wisdom from her symbol the serpent) are not to be trusted or listened to, for they defy God's commands and their words lead to folly and evil (cf. 1 Cor 14:33–35; 1 Tim 2:11–12); sexual awareness is the result of sin and is therefore tainted and dangerous (Gen 3:7, 21); men are required to rule over irresponsible women and ensure their obedience to God through submission to their husbands (cf. 1 Cor 11:3).

The Hebrew people living with their Goddess-worshiping neighbors could not have failed to understand the meaning contained within the myth. Centuries later, women today still feel the burden of blame and suspicion. As Stone writes, "My penitent, submissive position as a female was firmly established by page three of the nearly one thousand pages of the Judeo-Christian Bible."[13]

Christian Misogyny

Rooted in the Hebrew Scriptures and flourishing in a patriarchal culture, Christianity developed its own negative attitudes toward women and the old religion of the Goddess. At times subtle, at other times brutal, the movement was away from partnership and toward hierarchy, from feminine images of the Divine to strictly masculine ones. Despite Jesus' radical inclusion of women as friends and disciples and his refusal to treat them as second-rate, sinfully sexual, or stupid, his followers quickly established as orthodox an all-male priesthood, a masculine Trinity, and a theologically expressed aversion to women.

Thus Tertullian, a Christian theologian in the third century, described Eve as the gateway to the devil because, according to the Genesis myth, she first broke God's law and brought about the loss of original purity. He held her personally responsible for the death of Christ, and his general distrust and distaste of women was based on this rationale.

Origen, a theologian contemporary with Tertullian, wrote of the feminine and the corporeal as essentially one, and unworthy of God. He believed that God saw only the masculine and spiritual aspects of creation, since the Creator could surely not be expected to stoop so low as to regard the feminine and fleshly. St. Jerome, writing a century later, expressed this same equation of woman with sexuality and sin by reasoning that since Paul had written that it is well for a man not to touch a woman (1 Cor 7:1), then it must always be bad to touch a woman. Women were dangerously physical, inferior to men at best and destructive to their eternal souls at worst.

Virginity and celibacy therefore became elevated as spiritually more pure than marriage or sexual activity of any kind, and sexual sin was judged severely. Expressions of Christianity such as Gnosticism that gave women and men an equal place in the community, in liturgy, and in leadership, and that referred to the Godhead as "Mother" as well as "Father" were suppressed as heretical, and their sacred writings were destroyed.

Where the Wisdom tradition was brought to bear on Christology, with Christ seen as the incarnation of God's eternal and universal wisdom, the feminine word *Sophia* was replaced by the masculine *Logos*. And in Syria, where for four hundred years the word for Holy Spirit was *ruha*, a feminine word derived from the Hebrew *ruach*, and where the Holy Spirit was described as Mother, complementing the parental imagery of Father and Son in the Trinity, the association of feminine language with heresy led authors to assign masculine gender to the word—grammatical nonsense but evidence of the theological desire to defeminize the Divine.[14]

In the book of Acts, which relates the missionary journeys of Peter, Paul, and the other first-century Christian apostles, there is an account of a riot in Ephesus by the worshipers of the goddess Artemis (Diana), who were alarmed at the preaching of Paul against their goddess. Cynically presented by the author as economically motivated (he writes that the riot was instigated by a silversmith named Demetrius, who feared that the arrival of Christianity would dry up the sale of his silver shrines of Artemis), there is nevertheless a telling moment in the account when Demetrius says, "There is danger not only that this trade of ours may come into disrepute but also that the temple of the great goddess Artemis will be scorned, and she will be deprived of her majesty that brought all Asia and the world to worship her" (Acts 19:27). The town clerk quiets the crowd, who had gathered to chant "Great is Artemis of the Ephesians!" for two hours, and he disperses them successfully after reassuring them that Paul and his fellow missionaries are not temple robbers or blasphemers of the goddess, and that because it is undeniable that Ephesus is Artemis's sacred city, all will be well (Acts 19:35–41). History, however, proved Demetrius right and revealed the optimistic town clerk to be naive, for in 380 Emperor Theodosius closed down the temples of the Goddess not only in Ephesus but also in Eleusis and Rome. A century later the Parthenon, sacred temple to the Goddess in Athens for almost two thousand years, was converted into a Christian church.

Yet scholars such as Eisler have argued that the old religion of the Goddess did not die out. Despite the suppression of Goddess worship and the conversion of the Roman Empire into the Holy Roman Empire of Christendom, where Christianity became in the fourth century the official religion, the ancient wisdom and ways survived. As we have seen, Mary the mother of Jesus assumed many of the titles and functions of the Goddess; she became the Goddess's acceptable face within Christianity. People, especially in rural areas, continued to pray to her for their crops and animals, for healing, for safe delivery of their children. They continued to gather at the sacred times of the turning year: at the winter solstice (christianized and turned into the celebration of the birth of Jesus), when in the midst of darkness the return of the light was celebrated; at spring, when the Goddess Oestra (from whom we derive the Christian word Easter) was venerated for bringing her gifts of new life, fertility, and abundance; at summer and harvest, when the days were long, the fruits of the earth plentiful, and thanksgiving was offered to the Goddess; and at the hinge of autumn and winter, as darkness was returning and the spirits of the ancestors were believed to be very near and powerful.

This last festival of the Goddess cultures was called Samhein, but we know it now as Halloween. Originally a time when the people honored their forebears and the mysterious cycle of life, death, and regeneration, it became in Christian cultures a fearful time when the devil walked the earth and consorted with his own. It stands as a chilling example of the way in which the old religion of the Goddess was demonized by Christianity in one of the most brutal periods of Christian history, when the followers of the Goddess were known as witches and exterminated.

The Witch Hunts

"Something went terribly wrong with Christianity's original gospel of love," writes Eisler as she summarizes the conversion of Jesus' message of partnership, inclusiveness, and compassion into a system of domination, control, and violence. "How otherwise could such a gospel be used to justify all the torture, conquest and bloodletting carried out by devout Christians?"[15]

For a period of more than two hundred years medieval Europe was in the grip of a terrifying witch-craze. Numbers are debated; the lowest estimates are that several thousand were put to death on the charge of witchcraft in the mass persecutions of the fifteenth to seventeenth centuries; the highest estimates suggest that it may have been millions rather than thousands. Some of the victims were men and children, but the vast majority were women. At times whole communities were killed, reminiscent of the mass slaughters recorded in the Hebrew Scriptures of peoples who did not worship Yahweh.

The charge in this holocaust of women was always witchcraft, and neighbors, relatives, and friends were terrorized into denouncing one another, or arrested and tortured until they made the required "confessions" themselves. Their alleged crimes were of gathering to commune with the devil, celebrating black masses, murdering and devouring babies, making spells and curses of magic. But studies of the evidence that was painstakingly recorded at witch trials reveals a very different picture.

The women were mostly country dwellers; indeed the word "pagan" derives from the Latin *paganus*, meaning "one who lives in the country." They were uneducated by comparison with the ecclesiastical lawyers and clergy who tried them, and they practiced the earth-honoring seasonally based rites of the ancient religion. Many were herbalists and midwives who used their skills to control conception and relieve the pains of childbirth—two practices regarded as heretical by a system that viewed Eve's punishment as applying in perpetuity to all women, and that denied women even basic sexual and legal rights.

Single women, either widowed or never married, were regarded with deep sus-picion and hostility for their independence from male control. Along with women who owned land in their own name, and women who had a reputation for lacking the required docility to male neighbors and the clergy, they were those most at risk of being charged and tried. In inordinate numbers they were accused of causing male impotence, of consorting sexually with the devil, of having an "evil eye." Stripped of their possessions and forced to pay for their own imprisonment and trial, they were tortured then drowned, burned, or hanged.

The lurid "confessions" that "witches" made were standardized ones, written and widely distributed by the religious authorities in publications such as the infa-mous *Malleus Maleficarum*,[16] and repeated or signed under torture. They reveal the deep-seated misogyny and fear of sexuality that had developed in the church. The *Malleus*, for instance, stated that all witchcraft stemmed "from carnal lust which in women is insatiable." The confessions also depended upon the invention of a sadis-tic devil figure, based in part upon biblical texts, but also drawing on the old despised symbols of the Goddess—the serpent and her consort the horned bull.

Some have theorized that the witch hunts occurred during a period of enor-mous social upheaval in Europe, with warfare, famine, and plague causing havoc and threatening to destroy all stability. An enemy was needed, and the victims of the witch craze were social scapegoats. But it has also been argued that at times of crisis and chaos the wisdom of the old religion comes to the fore, in a resurgence of the quest for harmony rather than hierarchy, peace among peoples rather than power exerted over them.[17] This seems to be supported by the fact that in the period lead-ing up to the witch hunts there was a flowering in Europe of women's religious orders, the troubadour culture emerged, with its honoring of gentleness and roman-tic love, and mystics such as Julian of Norwich and Teresa of Avila were writing of God not as an all-powerful king but as a compassionate mother. The witch hunts may therefore have been in part the desperate and brutal reaction of the system, at both conscious and unconscious levels, to the reappearance of a long-suppressed feminine presence. As Rosemary Radford Ruether comments grimly: "By 1700, the persecutions gradually ended, not only because Enlightenment rationality made the myths of witches less acceptable but perhaps because they were no longer necessary. The clergy and male authorities had won."[18]

Searching for Home

The National Film Board of Canada has produced a trilogy of films on women's spirituality.[19] Several years ago I attended a viewing of two of them—*Goddess Remembered*, which describes the religion of the Goddess and the cultures that grew up around it for more than 20,000 years; and *Burning Times*, a dramatic documen-tary about the witch hunts. These films permanently changed me, for they gave me a new lens through which to see myself and my faith. It was as though I discovered that day that I was adopted; that long ago, before I could remember, I was taken from my mother and given to new parents who raised me and tried to make me become like them. My childhood and adolescence in the church had been happy and affirming; I had wanted to become a priest in order to give to others what had been given lovingly to me. But gradually I had become aware of something missing, something lost or broken, something that was considered dangerous.

Seeing the movies was like having flashbacks to a forgotten childhood. The spirituality that had the Goddess as its central symbol was strange to me, and yet it felt like home. While I had struggled to take my place in the church—finding my sense of vocation met with disapproval or dismissal—this other path recognized the spiritual gifts of women and respected them as bearers of the Divine. While I had scraped and scratched away the layers of patriarchy in the Bible and in Christian history in my quest for the feminine face of God, countless generations of my ancestors had known the Divine as Goddess, as she, with a thousand different names and faces. Throughout my theological studies and in my ministry and spiritual development I had worried that my unorthodox thoughts, doubts, and questions were heresy. Now I recognized that heresy had in fact often been "her-story," the attempt to rearticulate "his-story" and to find the Feminine Divine.

At some level, opponents of the ordination of women have known this. In an article that appeared in the British newspaper the *Times* on 23 May 1973, during the protracted ecclesiastical and public debate about women priests, the religious affairs correspondent reported that the Bishop of Exeter, Dr. Mortimer, had warned a church convocation in Canterbury that the ordination of women would be a shift toward pagan religions, in which priestesses were common. "And we all know the kinds of religions they were and are," Dr. Mortimer is reported to have said, adding that the church should be careful not to adapt to changes "in a sex obsessed culture."

There are several levels of irony in this small piece, not least the fact that we do *not* all know what the old pagan religions truly were. What we think we know is the result of a centuries-long smear campaign, so that pre-Christian religions are associated with unbridled sexuality, and sexuality in turn is associated with sin. Throw in the word "priestess" and the result is a frisson of fear and disgust, calculated to tip the scales against any possibility of women entering the Christian priesthood.

Language is powerful. I once asked my husband what mental image came to mind when he thought of the word "priest." He said he thought of a male figure in a black cassock, standing in a church in an attitude of solemnity. "What about when you think of the word 'priestess'"? I asked next. He thought for a while, then smiled and said he pictured a slim, beautiful woman dancing in flowing clothing in a sacred grove of trees. "And which image is more appealing?" was my final question, although I already knew what his answer would be. Yet we fear what we do not dare embrace.

A book opposing the ordination of women was published in 1984 in England under the title *What Will Happen to God?* with a picture on the cover of a crucified woman. The author, William Oddie, in a 26 October 1984 letter to the *Church Times*, wrote that his book was a theological examination of the issues raised by the "attack" on the revelation of God as Father by proponents of women's ordination, both the "eccentric radical feminists" as well as those "much nearer the centre of the Church's life." In another letter regarding Oddie's book, a female member of the General Synod (the governing body of the Church of England), herself a vehement opponent of women's ordination, wrote: "There can be few naive enough to believe that what these women want is simply a bit of the action. I am convinced that if women were to be ordained, it would not stop there. This will be one more step in undermining the doctrine of God given to us in the Bible."[20] Of course she is right. To recover the spiritual leadership of women in religion and to allow the Feminine Divine to reemerge is radically to reshape traditional Christian doctrine.

Feminist scholar Carol P. Christ, a classically trained theologian who turned her attention to the study of past and contemporary Goddess worship, has written of the effect on both the doctrine of God and the psychology and spirituality of women that "thea-logy"—the study of the Goddess—can have. In her essay "Why Women Need the Goddess" she explains:

> Religions centred on the worship of a male God create "moods" and "motivations" that keep women in a state of psychological dependence on men and male authority. . . . The simplest and most basic meaning of the symbol of Goddess is the acknowledgment of the legitimacy of female power as a beneficent and independent power.[21]

Starhawk, a Wiccan author, distinguishes between power as that which is exercised over others from an elevated, dominant, or transcendent position, and power as that which comes from within and enables others to become themselves empowered.[22] While God in patriarchal religions has typically been represented as almighty and transcendent, ruling over the world from heaven beyond, the Goddess by contrast is understood to be the Divine present in all things, immanent, nurturing, and connecting all of life together. Thus, "religion is a matter of relinking, with the divine within, and with her outer manifestations in all of the human and natural world."[23] It is not the submission of the will to a higher power, with all the metaphors of servant and lord, slave and master; rather, it is the joining of the will to the divine force or energy that creates and sustains all life. The metaphor is organic rather than hierarchical.

Carol Christ has written that the very word "Goddess" sends chills of recognition through women. As I experienced it, there is recognition of something ancient and yet familiar, long forgotten but somehow deeply life giving. At the same time there is the chilling knowledge that this is taboo and that the Goddess is dangerous. Just as the word "witch" is associated with satanic evil, and "priestess" with sexual cults, so the language and images of the Goddess are laden with negative connotations. When I began tentatively to pray to God as "she" in my private devotions, I did so with a strong pang of guilt. It was like a betrayal of the heritage into which I had been adopted and raised, or the furtive sending of a letter to the birth mother with the hope that the adoptive parents would not discover or object. Once I led a study group for students in which we focused on the religion of the Goddess and the feminine face of God in Judaism and Christianity. It was well attended, and led to many subsequent conversations in my office and over coffee. But I later discovered that some church leaders in town had warned their people not to attend the group, or any worship services conducted by me, since I was teaching unsound doctrine. The pressure to conform to the theological norm is strong, both internally and externally.

As I watched the film that described the witch hunts, I was well aware of the connection between the murderous church system then and the religious fundamentalist wing today, and I felt unsafe. The definers of orthodoxy hold enormous power. They state how the sacred texts of a tradition are to be interpreted, how the faith is to be practiced, how the Divine has been revealed—and to whom, and who is the heretic beyond the pale. There is a constant tension for people of faith (and in this context especially for women of faith) between exploring that faith, critiquing it, and wrestling with it in order to be able to enter it more deeply, on the one hand, and abandoning it, losing it, or being ejected from it, on the other. Again, the metaphor of the adopted child holds good: Is it possible to search for the birth mother, find her, and know her, while still living in the home of the adoptive parents? Or is it necessary first to leave home?

Radical feminists such as Naomi Goldenberg believe that Judaism and Christianity cannot be rehabilitated to become spiritually, psychologically, or societally healthy for women. They advocate a complete rejection of the adoptive parents as abusive and destructive. Goldenberg therefore sees feminism as "engaged in the slow execution of Christ and Yahweh,"[24] an execution that is necessary in order to free a culture that is presently "doomed to debase both women and nature because it has lost touch with the divine life force present in women and all natural life."[25]

Similarly, Mary Daly writes of the need to castrate God in order to discover the deity beyond patriarchy.[26] As her religious thought has developed she has abandoned her Judeo-Christian roots to articulate a post-Christian theology. Author Zsuzsanna E. Budapest supports an equally radical movement when she advocates self-blessing rituals for women to perform, as "a way of exorcizing the patriarchal policeman, cleansing the deep mind, and filling it with positive images of the strength and beauty of women" as an act of recovery from the destructive past.[27]

Ruether, however, with other feminist theologians who see themselves as reforming rather than jettisoning, executing, castrating, or exorcizing the traditions, points out that it is easy but misguided to see the feminist way of the Goddess as all good, and the path of the religions that came after it as totally destructive. While supporting the quest for female symbols of the Divine, she warns against a simplistic, biologically based dualism that sees females by their very nature "as loving, egalitarian, ecological and spontaneous," while males are seen "as alienated, dualistic, rapacious and destructive." The best way forward, as she sees it, is not to separate the masculine from the feminine and reject it, but to integrate the two paths and transform the present in new and liberating ways for all.

So as we feminist theologians and spiritual writers search for the Goddess and for our roots, we are trying both to conjure up a lost time and to create a new one. We are weaving together ancient wisdom and contemporary insights. We are reimaging God through the eyes, lives, and voices of those who were not heard previously in the Bible or in the formation of Christian doctrine. Playwright Monique Wittig expresses the task with urgent clarity: "There was a time when you were not a slave, remember that. You walked alone, full of laughter. . . . You say you have lost all recollection of it; remember! . . . You say there are no words to describe it; you say it does not exist. But remember! Make an effort to remember! Or failing that, invent!"[28] Call it golden age mythology, call it feminist invention, call it scholarly rediscovery, call it theological creativity. We need images of what can be. And whether we are yearning for something we have lost, or are struggling to create something the world has never known before, the passion remains. We are searching for a place to call home.

The Trouble with God

Traditional Judeo-Christian theology is lopsided. Ever since the failure of the Sky God to live at peace with the Goddess, when invasion and oppression made integration and partnership impossible, there has been a split deep at the heart of religious life. An either/or way of thinking has become normative: Either we worship the biblical God who is revealed as Father, or we water down the faith as woolly minded liberals or feminist heretics; either God reigns as King and patriarchy rules on earth, or the Goddess is Queen of Heaven and matriarchy wins the day; either you accept Jesus as Lord and Savior and all Scripture as inspired by God, or you are not a real Christian. Where integration fails, balance is lost. Theological dualism is the child of religious divorce.

It is evident within Christianity that a predominantly male-imaged God produces distortions within faith and practice. When God is named repeatedly and normatively as Father and Son, the maleness of divine images becomes established no matter how much lip service is paid to the notion that God is beyond gender or female images are included. A motherly father remains a father. Theologians such as Mary Daly, Dorothee Sölle, and Sallie McFague have demonstrated how limited and flawed the concept of the fatherhood of God is, when it stands as a fundamental doctrine of faith unbalanced by equally strong concepts from female experience.

Daly describes this lone Father God as "the God-Father," deliberately using the Mafia image to illustrate the associations with power, violence, and machismo. This is the God who inspires not love but fear. In the words of Sölle, writing in the aftermath of Hitler's "Fatherland" with its death camps, this is the God "whose prime need is to subjugate, whose greatest fear is equality."[29] This God describes himself in the Hebrew Scriptures as "a jealous God." He fears the possibility of human beings becoming like himself (Gen 3:22–23; 11:6–7). He strikes dead any who dare to approach too close (Exod 19:21–24; 2 Sam 6:6–7) or any who displease him (e.g., Acts 5:1–5). Sölle maintains that the title "Father" has lost any theological innocence it might once have had, and is associated now with a sexist, technocratic, male-dominated society, and with "roaring, shooting and giving orders."[30] She sees a focus on God as Father leading to a culture where obedience is the primary requirement, and where a superior power renders humankind powerless, pessimistic, and fatalistic. It is a culture where suffering is seen as God's will, since he is in control. To question the workings of this divine authority is to be rebellious and sinful.

Jesus, it is pointed out in defense, spoke of a loving Father. Yet even the Gospels contain parables of hell and judgment that are sadistic in their violence and retribution. Matthew's Gospel, for instance, concludes the parable of the Unforgiving Servant this way:

> Then his lord summoned [the slave] and said to him, "You wicked slave! I forgave you all that debt because you pleaded with me. Should you not have had mercy on your fellow slave, as I had mercy on you?" And in anger his lord handed him over to be tortured until he would pay his entire debt. So my heavenly Father will also do to every one of you, if you do not forgive your brother or sister from your heart. (Matt 18:32–35)

This same heavenly Father, when portrayed in parables as a landowner, a king, a master of slaves, or a judge, condemns those who do wrong to be put to death, broken to pieces, crushed, tied up, thrown into outer darkness, cut to pieces, and consigned to the place of weeping and gnashing of teeth (see Matt 21:41, 44; 22:13; 24:51; 25:30, and parallels).

For victims of abusive human fathers, the cult of fear is all too familiar. When this theology of divine violence and punishment is extended to interpret the death of Jesus, the Son who takes on himself the death penalty required by his Father for the sins of the world, the intended message of divine love becomes sickeningly associated with child abuse, scapegoating, and sadomasochism.

When we use human metaphors to describe God, God becomes associated inevitably with our human experience. The word "Father" (or "Mother") to an abused child may conjure up memories of fear and pain, not love. It is precisely because language is so powerfully evocative that religious metaphors matter. Their effect cannot be controlled by insisting that one should think of God only as a *loving* Father, a *merciful* judge, and so on; instead, their use must be consciously balanced and relativized. As absolutes, as exclusive, as ultimate truth, they have the power to destroy.

When God is male, not only is the male tantamount to a god in a sexist society, as Daly has written, but God is also associated (because of the history of male activity) with militarism, force, and violent conflict. Thus, disciples become "soldiers of Christ," mission becomes bloody crusade, the newly baptized are told to "fight manfully under [the] banner [of Christ],"[31] the spiritual life is seen as a constant inner battle between forces of good and evil, and the end of the world is pictured in apocalyptic Technicolor as a cosmic battle between those forces, resulting in the total destruction of earth.

A dualistic paradigm divides reality, both human and divine, into two opposing camps. On one side is God, spirit, the sacred, heaven, salvation, light, goodness, reason, the mind, the masculine; on the other is the devil, matter, the profane, earth, damnation, darkness, evil, irrationality, the body, the feminine. Like oppositional forces pulling everything one way or the other, a dualistic theology is constantly sorting, rarely integrating. Out of this paradigm come relationships not based on an "I-Thou" concept of mutuality, but founded on "I-It," subject-object, superior-inferior polarity.

In the end, the trouble with God as he has been conceived in this dualistic culture is that he stands alone as a being transcendent and supreme, ruling in aloof omnipotence according to a fixed and changeless plan. The Christian doctrine of the love of God is bowed down under the weight of conflicting teachings about God's inscrutable will, his requirement of obedience, and his frightening punishments. Our lopsided theology caricatures and distorts the Divine, causing people to abandon their faith because it is abhorrent or merely unbelievable.

Jürgen Moltmann writes of "the distress of the male Ruler-God" who is

> the Almighty, the Lord, the Absolute. . . . He determines everything; nothing influences him. He is incapable of suffering [and therefore of love]. . . . He is defined only by his function as ruler and proprietor of the world. Who he himself is remains unknown. Thus patriarchy divides, separates, and isolates God. A God who is no more than "the Almighty" is not a God but a monster.[32]

In response to this, Christian charismatic and evangelical movements have stressed the personal relationship between the believer and God, with an emphasis on highly emotional piety. Bumper stickers insist that God loves you, but underlying the wide smile is the qualifier: You must repent and be saved, or spend eternity in hell. As a church bulletin board I once saw expressed it, with the thin disguise of humor, "Where will you spend eternity: smoking or non-smoking?" God's love is, after all, conditional; or it is the psychotic distortion of love that goes hand in hand with rage and violence.

Saving God

For years I made excuses for God. I tried to make the jagged pieces of traditional theology fit together into a smooth picture of the God I loved. But the more I read, the more I saw of the wounds inflicted by Christianity past and present, and the more I experienced the rejection of myself as female by the church, the harder it became. I was doing increasingly elaborate theological gymnastics to make sense of God.

It grieved me that close friends and family members had given up on God. My father, a Scottish Presbyterian by upbringing, had a Celtic heart of deep emotion under a dour facade. He had been taught that God was both all-loving and all-powerful, and he could not understand why there was therefore so much innocent and undeserved pain in the world. His medical work took him to post-Stalinist Russia several times, and I remember him weeping as he told us of visiting with his Russian hosts the vast cemeteries where their massacred families were buried. As a newly qualified doctor he had seen tuberculosis wards full of young lives wasting away. Working with the World Health Organization toward the end of his career, he traveled to developing countries and witnessed the massive toll on human life through the simple lack of clean water, adequate food, and basic health care. If God is in control, he would ask, why is the world in such a mess? I could not answer his questions, or save God from his angry atheism.

Lesbian and gay friends carried other wounds. An inclusive gospel for all, whether male or female, slave or free, Jew or Gentile (Gal 3:28) nevertheless did not include them. The message from liberation theology of God's preferential option for the poor and oppressed stopped short of them. They learned in church that God loved them but that their sexual orientation was sinful, an abomination. They heard biblical passages in which the penalty for their kind was death (see Lev 20:13). They tried to change themselves, they begged God to heal them and make them acceptably heterosexual, they crippled their emotional lives by cutting themselves off from intimacy. In the face of the experiences of these friends, my theology became pretzel shaped as I twisted it around to try to make it palatable.

There have been so many others whose pain and questions have shaken the box in which God was imprisoned: the bereaved, with their experience of the absence of God; survivors of abuse, with their appalling legacy of shame, needing to be told not that they are guilty sinners in God's eyes but that life can be good and love can be trusted; people of other faiths and none, showing me that Christianity is not the only way to find peace, goodness, and meaning. I need a theology that fits the facts and does not wound.

My discovery of the feminine face of God was the first step in dismantling the box and setting God free. My search for the Goddess enabled me to begin to envision a different way of believing, worshiping, and living, in which the Divine was not transcendent and wholly Other and in which a pyramid of hierarchical relationships did not flow from heaven to earth. I began to see oneness as the root metaphor—oneness with God, with each other, with all of creation.

Jungian author Carol S. Pearson has personified the stages of inner psychospiritual development as the journeys of the Innocent, the Orphan, the Warrior or Martyr, the Wanderer, and the Magician.[33] The Innocent is like a young child at home, accepting and uncritical. But the Orphan realizes that she is ultimately alone, and has to leave home to find herself. She may adopt the role of Warrior at first, battling her way in reaction to the rules and norms that surround her, or she may choose the Martyr's path, submitting to the will and force of others. As Wanderer she moves beyond that choice into unmarked territory, where she neither reacts against nor submits to but learns to identify her own voice, will, and power. Finally, she enters the stage of Magician, where she has discovered the transformative energy within and beyond herself, and knows how to live by it.

As Innocent, I loved to be with my mother as she knelt and prayed in the old stone churches of England. I breathed in the incense and the prayer and I felt at home. I admired the parish priest who cared enough to take an interest in me and treat me seriously as I was growing up. I wanted to be just like him, to dedicate my life to God and to serve his people in his church.

As Orphan I realized that what I had to offer was not wanted by the church. I heard voices of rejection and contempt. Male students at the theological college I was about to attend performed a skit in which they likened the ordination of a woman to the ordination of a dog. My parish priest admitted that he himself did not believe women should be priests. Incredulous at first, I began to experience the anger, hurt, and sense of loss caused by patriarchy.

Searching for a place to call home, I encountered the ancient religion of the Goddess and, at the same time, the ugly history of its suppression. The Warrior feminist in me fought against the domination system that was everywhere. I experienced moments of inner rage that gripped and terrified me. There were times when I wanted nothing more to do with men and their world. Meanwhile, the Martyr in me felt overwhelmed with powerlessness and slid toward cynicism and depression. Working as a deaconess, a second-class citizen in ministry, and witnessing the Church of England vote over and over again not to accept the priestly ministry of women, the sense of certainty I had had in my vocation began to leak away.

As Wanderer I left England and made a new home with David in Canada. I was ordained a priest in the Anglican Church of Canada, but discovered that my journey could not end there. I am not content, as the author of the letter to the *Church Times* predicted in 1984, with "simply a bit of the action." I want to serve a God who does not wear the face of patriarchy. I want to paint into the picture the colors of the Goddess. So I sit at my desk and write, not knowing where this journey will end or who I will be at its conclusion. But the quest has its own imperative and momentum, and I do not travel alone.

In finding one's own voice, will, and transforming energy, theology becomes not a systematic product of revelation from beyond, but at least in part a process of bringing forth truth from experience. Women have not been encouraged to do this for several thousand years, so the effort to tell, to remember, to create, is a hard and painful one. But in the process of naming ourselves and our experiences we can unexpectedly encounter the Divine. "I found god in myself," writes poet and playwright Ntosake Shange, "and I loved her, I loved her fiercely."[34]

Notes

1. Merlin Stone, *When God Was a Woman* (San Diego: Harvest/Harcourt Brace, 1976).

2. See, for example, the writings of James Mellaart and Marija Gimbutas.

3. Stone, *When God Was a Woman*, xx.

4. Ibid., 22.

5. Riane Eisler, *The Chalice and the Blade* (New York: Harper and Row, 1987).

6. Ibid., 23.

7. Ibid., 31.

8. Ibid., 36.

9. Marija Gimbutas, "The First Wave of Eurasian Steppe Pastoralists," *Journal of Indo-European Studies* 5 (Winter 1977): 281.

10. Eisler, *Chalice and the Blade*, 84.

11. Joseph Campbell, *The Masks of God: Occidental Mythology* (New York: Viking Press, 1964), 17.

12. See, e.g., Exod 34:13; Deut 7:5; 16:21; Judg 6:25; 2 Chron 34:7.

13. Stone, *When God Was a Woman*, 6.

14. See Sebastian Brock, "The Holy Spirit as Feminine in Early Syriac Literature," in *After Eve* (ed. Janet Martin Soskice; London: Marshall Pickering, 1990), 73–88.

15. Eisler, *Chalice and the Blade*, 131.

16. "The Hammer of Witches," a work written by the Inquisitors ca. 1487 describing the alleged practices of witchcraft.

17. Eisler, *Chalice and the Blade*, 140–42.

18. Rosemary Radford Ruether, "Misogynism and Virginal Feminism in the Fathers of the Church," in *Religion and Sexism* (ed. Ruether; New York: Simon and Schuster, 1974), 172.

19. Donna Read, "Women and Spirituality," National Film Board, Canada.

20. Frances Flatman, letter to *The Church Times*, 26 October 1984.

21. Carol P. Christ, "Why Women Need the Goddess," in *Womanspirit Rising* (ed. Carol P. Christ and Judith Plaskow; San Franciso: Harper Collins, 1992), 275, 277.

22. Wicca is a pagan Goddess religion, described by Starhawk as being based on the core principles of immanence, interconnection, and community. See Starhawk, *The Spiral Dance* (New York: Harper and Row, 1979), 10–11.

23. Starhawk, *Spiral Dance*, 23.

24. Naomi Goldenberg, *Changing of the Gods* (Boston: Beacon, 1979), 4.

25. Ibid., 105.

26. Mary Daly, *Beyond God the Father* (Boston: Beacon, 1973), 19.

27. Zsuzsanna E. Budapest, "Self Blessing Ritual," in *Womanspirit Rising* (ed. Carol P. Christ and Judith Plaskow; San Francisco: Harper Collins, 1992), 272.

28. Monique Wittig, *Les Guerilleres* (trans. David LeVay; New York: Avon Books, 1971), 89.

29. Dorothee Sölle, *The Strength of the Weak* (Philadelphia: Westminster, 1984), 97.

30. Dorothee Sölle, "Paternalistic Religion as Experienced by Woman," in J.-B. Metz and E. Schillebeeckx Concilium 143, no. 3 (Edinburgh: T&T Clark, 1981), 72.

31. Book of Common Prayer (Toronto: Anglican Book Centre, 1962), 528.

32. Elisabeth Moltmann-Wendell and Jürgen Moltmann, "Becoming Human in New Community," in Constance F. Parvey, ed., *The Community of Women and Men in the Church* (Geneva: World Council of Churches, 1983), 33.

33. See Carol S. Pearson, *The Hero Within* (San Francisco: HarperSanFrancisco, 1986).

34. Ntosake Shange, *For Coloured Girls Who Have Considered Suicide When the Rainbow Is Enuf* (New York: Macmillan, 1975), 63.

CHAPTER 3
Loss of Faith: Rethinking

Theology and Disbelief

"Systematic theology" was the title given to a large portion of the theology I studied as an undergraduate. It appeals to the rational desire to have the doctrines of Christianity laid out, examined, labeled, and understood as clearly as organs on a dissection table. Learning the thinking of the major theologians in the West (mostly Protestant, many German, none female), I wrote papers on the nature of God, the meaning of the death of Christ, the problem of evil, the incarnation, and so on. Theology in that context was a pleasingly complex intellectual process of bringing together biblical texts, academic reflection, and logical deduction, and presenting it with sufficient finesse to receive a good grade.

Then, as a newly ordained deaconess, I conducted a funeral for a woman who had died suddenly at age thirty, and my carefully constructed theological house of cards fell flat. She had been an ordinary woman going about her life until a diagnosis of cancer had put her in hospital. Two weeks later she was dead. Her husband and family were devastated. Nothing had prepared them for this. Worse, their view of the world and of God's loving hand in it told them that this could not have happened, should not have happened. As a minister of religion, I felt like God's ambassador, but I could not explain why their loved one had died. After one of my meetings with the family I drove out of town a little way, parked at the top of a windswept hill, and rested my head on the steering wheel to weep tears of desolation. I was crying for the family, but also for the death of my image of God.

It was not that I had been unaware of the reality of suffering before then, but somehow I had guarded my theology from that awareness. I had kept the two in separate containers, and used subtle theological arguments to explain away the problem of evil. But standing in front of a congregation of mourners, none of whom had had the dubious benefit of reading Augustine, Karl Barth, or the other classic theologians, my words sounded hollow and comfortless in the face of such anguish.

As my first Christmas in ministry drew near, I experienced a profound loss of faith that paralyzed and terrified me. God seemed no more than a nice idea, which had now been shown to be a sham. The traditional understanding of suffering as something God, out of love, permits in order for us to draw closer to God and be purified like gold ore in a hot fire seemed cruel and unnecessary. Did the woman deserve to die? Did her family deserve to lose her? Were they to learn some deep lesson from her death? Was it really God's will that she die? Or was her death merely a random, meaningless event in a world where cancer cells develop and spread arbitrarily? If so, what did that say about God?

It was not my choice to walk away from the traditional theological answers to these questions; I simply did not believe them anymore. They made God a deity I no longer wanted to worship. A God who permitted cancer (or murder, or starvation, or war, or earthquakes), for whatever ultimate purpose, was not a God I could love. "The value of a god must be open to test," J. Mitchell writes in *The God I Want*. "A worthwhile god must prove himself by changing the rules about suffering."[1]

Crash-Test Theology

The pain of our experience of being alive is the anvil on which our theology must be hammered out, if it is to be a theology of truth and reality and not a system of wishful thinking or an abstract mental construction. Pain, loss, doubt, and anger all offer a challenge to religious thought and spirituality. Dare we construct and reconstruct our faith in accordance with what we know and experience, the worst as well as the best? Or do we hunker down under the protection of an unchanging faith that was handed down to us, which may be internally consistent and beautifully systematic but is unrelated to the raw stuff of our lives?

This is in essence the anguish of Job. A righteous man is afflicted with the loss of children, possessions, and health (Job 1:13–2:8), and his belief in the righteousness of God breaks down in the face of this injustice. He protests:

> Though I am innocent . . .
> > I must appeal for mercy to my accuser.
> If I summoned him and he answered me,
> > I do not believe that he would listen to my voice. . . .
>
> He destroys both the blameless and the wicked.
> When disaster brings sudden death,
> > he mocks at the calamity of the innocent. (Job 9:15–16, 22–23)

Job's friends attempt to comfort him by reasserting the old beliefs that we get what we deserve, that the innocent are rewarded and the guilty punished. They warn him that to question God's righteousness is to sin further:

> For you say, "My conduct is pure,
>   and I am clean in God's sight."
> But O, that God would speak,
>   and open his lips to you,
> and that he would tell you the secrets of wisdom! . . .

> Know then that God exacts of you less than your guilt deserves.
> (Job 11:4–6)

> You are doing away with the fear of God,
>   and hindering meditation before God. . . .
> Why does your heart carry you away,
>   and why do your eyes flash,
> so that you turn your spirit against God
>   and let such words go out of your mouth? (Job 15:4, 12–13)

"Agree with God," they urge (22:21), and all will be well. But Job persists in his claim that he is righteous and, like many others, that he is suffering innocently. He rages at God for the injustices of life, and, according to scholars who believe that the book of Job originally concluded without the voice of God answering from the whirlwind, his words end in bitter loneliness.

The problem of evil, and specifically the problem of undeserved suffering, is the crash test for theology. Job's friends represent those who hold fast to their picture of God as supreme and all-knowing, dispensing reward and punishment according to humanity's guilt and sin—even though in maintaining this view they inevitably have to find Job guilty, since he is so afflicted. Job himself stands for those who cannot accept a theology that runs counter to their own most visceral experience. At the risk of being accused of godlessness, they rage against a God they can no longer believe in.

The Death of God

To summarize the image of God that finally collapsed for me, its central feature is power: God is omnipotent, in control of all events, ruling the universe from beyond it, permitting suffering for a greater good, intervening occasionally to save the faithful, allowing evil its day but ultimately triumphing over it. Words such as *immutable* (unchanging), *impassible* (incapable of suffering), and *omniscient* (knowing and therefore determining all things) have been used to describe this God. Drawn from concepts in Greek philosophy, this theology describes a deity who is perfect in every way, such perfection including his very existence. But it is a cold, comfortless perfection. He is the God of patriarchy, the God "who corresponds to what men would like to be."[2]

In reaction to this doctrine of God, the "death of God" theologians in Europe and North America wrote in the 1960s and 70s of the need for theological deconstruction: "The God seen as a person, making the world, manipulating some people towards good, condemning other people to damnation—the objectified God in other words—this is the God many have declared to be dead today. This is the God who must disappear, so that we may remake our thinking and our speaking about him."[3] Taking seriously the post-Enlightenment critique of religion by writers such as Blake, Hegel, Kierkegaard, Dostoevsky, Nietzsche, and Weil—writers sometimes dismissed as atheist or anti-Christian—the "death of God" theologians struggled to free faith from anachronistic metaphors and unworkable thought forms. They acknowledged the uncertainty of their endeavor, departing as they were from accepted theological methods and assumptions. Their process was courageous and vulnerable, because they refused to cling to any assumptions or presuppositions about God, even at the risk of concluding that there was no place left in their world-view or theology for God. Central to their stripping away of theological deadwood was the problem of suffering—its tragic and horrifying reality, and its ability to shine a merciless light on any view of God based on wishful thinking. Their theology had an honesty and realism to it which I knew I needed. It did not furnish me with a new systematic set of beliefs about God, but it took seriously my questions and verbalized my sense that my old image of God had to die—or had already died.

God with Us

If the "death of God" theologians raised some of the questions facing traditional theology, feminist theologians have provided some of the answers. Most importantly, because God in feminist thought is not perceived as being in a position of omnipotent control beyond the universe, the starting point is entirely different and the possibilities flow from there along very different channels.

While God in classical (patriarchal) thought is transcendent, all-powerful, and impassible, in feminist theology God is immanent, vulnerable, and passionate. The defining images are not ruler, king, or judge, but lover, parent, woman in labor. God is intimately and everywhere present with us, in suffering as in joy. Further, God can be said to suffer *with* us, since love inevitably involves pain—the pain of empathy, vulnerability, risk. The biblical metaphor of the woman in labor is a profound image of hope. The whole of creation is, as Paul writes, "groaning in labor pains" toward a time of freedom and glory, and God as Spirit labors with us, "with sighs too deep for words" (Rom 8:22, 26). God is not remote or only our help and support, but is actually involved in the birthpangs of bringing life and goodness into the world.

Death of God theology buries the distant God who sits on a throne in heaven watching over a world that runs according to a predestined plan. Feminist theology celebrates the God who is with us. Like Jesus weeping for his friend Lazarus and grieving over the faithless intransigence of Jerusalem, God weeps with us in our pain and refuses to abandon us.

This shift from the almighty Father to the compassionate companion was the first step for me through my crisis of faith. Although my reading and exploration of the motherhood of God had earlier opened a door to new ways of conceptualizing the Divine, I had never before experienced a door slamming shut on the old concepts. Now I knew that I could not simply balance the almighty Father with the compassionate Mother. The whole language and thinking of God as powerful and in control had to go.

Initially all I could do was embrace a weak God, an impotent, kindly God who has been caricatured as "old and soft and mellow and pitying, more like a grandfather than a father, but most like a shaky old grandmother."[4] Phrases such as "the foolishness of God" and "the crucified God" used by contemporary theologians such as John Taylor and Jürgen Moltmann aroused images I could hold on to. In my personal reading, searching for people of faith who might be at home on the terrain I was stumbling through, I came across authors who spoke of God as coming to us in our misery and pain and simply weeping with us, as mired in the mess with us—not fixing it but sharing it.[5] Their words lessened my loneliness and comforted me. The fact that they still identified themselves as Christian gave me hope, too, at a time when I was questioning my religious belonging because of my doubts.

For my first Christmas sermon, from the confusion and disturbance of letting go of the almighty Father, I preached about God as Emmanuel: God with us. It has become a mantra since then, an anchor to root me, a theological minimum. God-with-us does not provide all the answers or take away the pain. God-with-us is, to some, an outrageously pale shadow of Almighty God. And God-with-us provokes new questions about the purpose of prayer.

While I was at theological college preparing for ministry as a deaconess, the infant son of an ordinand and his wife became seriously ill. Prayers were said for the child during our twice daily worship services, but as the weeks passed a theological (and very heated) debate developed among the students. On one side were the theologically liberal, who did not believe God intervenes in the world or performs miracles. They had demythologized God, and saw the Bible stories of miraculous healings as pious inventions not to be taken literally. So they prayed for the child, but without expectation of anything miraculous happening. On the other side were the theologically conservative, who believed that with sufficient faith and prayer

God could and indeed would intervene to heal. They passionately believed in miracles, but feared that the presence in church of the cynical liberals might impede God's intervention. When the child became well they felt vindicated.

Yet the concept around which both camps argued was that of divine intervention, a concept which implies that initially or normally God is not present but has to be brought into the picture. Its starting point is divine distance. In contrast, a theology based on the faith that God is always and everywhere with us does not approach prayer from the same premise. If God is with us, we do not need to plead for divine intervention or stand aloof from it as a myth. Instead, prayer becomes opening to an encounter with this present God. This was made strikingly clear to me several years later when I was at the bedside of a dying man with his family and two other priests. It was another tragic death, occurring too soon, too young. Ray was a gentle, loving man with many gifts, but now he was close to death. Someone articulated the age-old question, "Where is God now?" The older priest replied, "God is right here, with Ray." He spoke the words not as a cliché but as a fundamental truth, and in that moment the room became a sacred place, as God's presence filled our awareness. Ray died, but God was there.

From this perspective it also becomes clear that God is not for some and against others, like a tribal deity championing his favored army. Love does not have favorites, nor can it rejoice in the destruction of any of its beloved. A Jewish legend in the Talmud tells of God's grief at the drowning of the Egyptian army in the sea as Moses and the people of Israel escaped to freedom: "In that very hour when the Egyptians were drowned in the sea, the angels wanted to praise God with a hymn. God, however, praised be the holy name, shouted, 'Human beings created by me are dying in the sea, and you want to rejoice?'"[6]

God's infinite capacity to love causes God also to suffer. In Christian history the grief of the Father at the death of the Son has only occasionally been portrayed, as opposed to the more common representation of the Father grimly requiring the death. And the suggestion that the Father suffers has been labeled as heresy (patripassianism), as though to suffer is to be imperfect or fall short in some way. But the opposite is true: To love is to open oneself to suffering, whether one is human or divine, and to embrace vulnerability instead of control.

Theologian Frances Young builds on the concept of God sharing the birthpangs of creation's struggle by suggesting that the death of Jesus was not a sacrifice for sin or an appeasement of a wrathful God, but was the act of a God who "takes responsibility for the appalling consequences of his act of creation."[7] The cross then becomes most deeply a sign of God's vulnerable love. In a real sense it is God who is crucified, not God who demands a death. Paul writes that Jesus "emptied himself" of his divinity in order to become human and be obedient to God (Phil 2:6–8). We may extend that image and speak of God being emptied of transcendent power, as we reimage the Divine. "We have chosen to live with the dangers of the impotence or weakness of God, rather than with the dangers of his power," writes death-of-God theologian William Hamilton, "for we believe that this was God's choice in the crucifixion."[8]

This radical reinterpretation of the meaning of Jesus' crucifixion is a critical part of feminist theology. It dismantles the idea of a God up in heaven sending the Son down to earth to die. It challenges the view of the death of Jesus as part of some sort of transaction with the devil. It does not cast humanity in the role of the accused, condemned by the Father but then delivered by the Son. Nor does it use what has been called "the most pernicious form of emotional blackmail"[9] by stating that because Jesus loved us enough to die for us we should love him in return. Most significantly, it does not take for granted that there is a huge gulf fixed between us and God because of sin; quite the opposite, God is inseparable from us and we from God. This is not a theological invention by feminists, but is a biblical theme, a counterweight to the texts of alienation and separation. Thus, the pessimistic prophecies of doom in the book of Revelation, for example, where all but a chosen few are destined to destruction (see, e.g., Rev 20:15), are turned upside down in light of the psalmist's statement of God's inescapable presence:

> Where can I go from your spirit?
>> Or where can I flee from your presence?
> If I ascend to heaven, you are there;
>> if I make my bed in Sheol, you are there.
> If I take the wings of the morning
>> and settle at the farthest limits of the sea,
> even there your hand shall lead me,
>> and your right hand shall hold me fast.
> If I say, "Surely the darkness shall cover me,
>> and the light around me become night,"
> even the darkness is not dark to you;
>> the night is as bright as the day,
>> for darkness is as light to you. (Ps 139:7–12)

We in God and God in Us

New insights into the person of Christ flow from an understanding of God's indwelling presence with us. Traditionally stated, the doctrine of the incarnation begins with the problematic separation of humanity from God. As the bridge across this chasm, Jesus Christ "came down from heaven," states the Nicene Creed, "and was made [hu]man." In him humanity and divinity met, not as a hybrid demi-god or as an exceptionally wise and good holy man, but as "perfect God; perfect Man . . .

who although he be God and Man, yet he is not two, but is one Christ," as the Athanasian Creed declares. Divinity and humanity are in essence totally distinct, coming together only in Christ through the miracle of the incarnation—literally, "the coming into flesh" of God. It is the familiar association of humanity with such concepts as flesh, earth, below, and sin, whereas divinity is on an opposite pole together with spirit, heaven, above, and sanctity. Thus, Christ is perceived as unique because he alone, during his earthly life, united God and humanity. He is therefore the "only Son of the Father," and his disciples seek to be Christlike but can never share his divine nature.

From a feminist perspective there are several problems with this Christology. First and most obviously, it lends itself all too easily to the notion that since this unique incarnation of the divine was male, there is something inherently more godly about maleness than femaleness. If God chose in which gender to enter human flesh, the choice is evident and leaves the unchosen gender inferior. As Origen said, "God does not stoop to look upon what is feminine." There is an implicit assumption that the more appropriate "container" for divinity is male, and we find ourselves back at the creation story with Adam made in God's image and Eve a secondary afterthought made from a spare rib. Similarly, when the Athanasian Creed declares that the incarnation took place "not by conversion of Godhead into flesh, but by taking of Manhood into God," some have argued that femaleness was not "taken into God" and is therefore not saved. Some, on the basis of this, have even concluded that women are without souls. Incarnational doctrine can thus become an easy tool of misogyny.

But another problem centers around the assumption that humanity and divinity are essentially different, like oil and water, or like an artist and a painting. The biblical image is of a potter and the clay: God is subject, humanity object (see, e.g., Ps 2:9; Lam 4:2; Rom 9:21). When the two are made entirely distinct there is no room for any concept of the divine presence within all human beings, and the sense of connection with the God who birthed us and breathed life into us is wholly obscured. Dualism denies union and sees the incarnation as an isolated experience in the history of the world.

When the starting point is not separation but oneness, however, the incarnation reveals an eternal truth: God is and always has been with us, and we are in God, the one in whom "we live and move and have our being" (Acts 17:28). So Christ is not, in theologian Norman Pittenger's words, an "outlandish anomaly but rather the classic instance of divine Activity in human expression." Christ represents "what God is always up to vis-a-vis humanity."[10] "The point," says Mary Daly, "is not to deny that a revelatory event took place in the encounter with the person of Jesus. Rather, it is to affirm that the creative presence of [God] can be revealed at every historical moment, in every person and culture."[11]

It is precisely because humanity and divinity are not mutually exclusive opposites that Jesus was a real human being and yet revealed God. His uniqueness lies not in a miraculous birth or supernatural powers, but in his ability to be so closely united to God, open to the breath of the Spirit, that his very being was permeated with the Divine. In *The Gospel according to Jesus*, poet and author Stephen Mitchell uses the analogy of Jesus as a window, so open and clear that it lets the sunlight stream through unimpeded. This is, in fact, what a window is meant for. Similarly, our calling is to clear away the murk that obscures the light (ignorance, fear, greed, apathy) so that we too may reveal the sun.

Inching forward more by instinct than by design, I preached a sermon to my fellow ordinands (an intimidating experience each of us had to undergo) in which I used the imagery of the ocean and a drop of water to represent the nature of God's relationship to humanity. At an intuitive level, despite my five years of theological training rather than because of it, I sensed the truth in this image: that our existence is derived entirely from God, who is our source, our being and our end. God is with us and within us, and we are in God.

The theological term for this is *panentheism*. It affirms that God (*theos*) is in (*entos*) all things (*pan*), and all things are in God. It is different from *pantheism*, which says that everything is God, with no sense of divine reality beyond nature. And it is decidedly different from *theism*, which accepts that there is a God but regards this deity as nonpersonal, distant, and disengaged from life after the initial act of creation. Panentheism stresses the connectedness of all things in God and the sacredness of creation.

In its Christian form panentheism recognizes what theologian Matthew Fox calls the "Cosmic Christ," divinity incarnated in all things. The Christian mystics knew this truth experientially through prayer and vision, and expressed it vividly. Mechtild of Magdeburg wrote:

> I who am Divine am truly in you.
> I can never be sundered from you:
> However far we be parted,
> never can we be separated.
> I am in you and you are in Me.[12]

And Hildegard of Bingen described God thus:

> I ignite the beauty of the plains,
> I sparkle the waters,
> I burn in the sun, and the moon, and the stars. . . .
>
> I adorn all the earth.[13]

Similarly, Julian of Norwich wrote of Christ that he is the one "in whom we are all enclosed and he in us."[14]

There is a profound optimism at the heart of this path, for instead of viewing humanity as basically wicked, with an innate tendency to draw away from God when left unguided, like oil separating from water, a spirituality that celebrates the oneness of all things in God and God in all things tends to regard humans as inherently capable of great goodness—even, as the theologians of the Eastern Orthodox tradition have taught, *capax Dei*, "capable of God." Thomas Aquinas (1225–1274) expressed this view in the following sayings:

> Every creature participates in some way in the likeness of the Divine Essence.
>
> We are meant to become more like God.
>
> The Son of God became human in order that humans might become gods and become the children of God.[15]

To affirm that I am in God, and God is in me, is to break down the dualistic thinking that exiles God to a different plane of existence called heaven. We no longer live conceptually in a three-level universe, with earth our mortal home and hell below us or heaven above as our two alternative destinies. Yet much of our theology has taken this for granted in its tendency to rank, order, and separate. It has been deeply skeptical of the ability of things "of the earth," "the world," or "the flesh" to reveal God. Indeed, these are often equated with the realm of the devil. In the Anglican baptismal rite, for example, as it was used (and continues to be used) from the time of the Reformation until the liturgical revisions of the last two decades, a period of more than four hundred years, the priest prays that the child to be baptized "may have power and strength to have victory, and to triumph against the devil, the world, and the flesh." Immediately after the baptism the priest makes the sign of the cross on the child's forehead as a sign that she or he is now Christ's, and is "manfully to fight under his banner against sin, the world, and the devil."[16] The language is conflictual: Earth is our temporary home, a dangerous, troublesome place, to be passed through with as little contamination as possible, battling against its sinful lusts and pomps until victory is won and heaven arrived at after death. The idea that the world might be loved, the body's wisdom trusted, the earth respected, is wholly absent here.

Countering this religious dualism that always lends itself to fundamentalism, feminist theology seeks a unitive approach. It challenges oppositional thinking, and it refuses an otherworldly focus for religion. At the same time, it explores a rich variety of religious imagery and metaphor, because diversity is seen as a gift and not a threat. When the truth is embraced that God's presence is in all that is, everything has the potential for becoming an epiphany, a revelation of God, not just the officially sanctioned revelations authorized by the church. A dying man, an infant at the breast, a tree growing on a rock, a mountain view—all can be epiphanies that bring God back from exile in heaven to intimate presence with us, around us, beyond us, between us.

Sophia-Spirit: God as Being and Becoming

In her critique of patriarchal theology, Mary Daly writes of God as "Be-ing," and echoes God's self-naming in the book of Exodus as "I Am Who I Am" or "I Will Be Who I Will Be." God is always "in the act of," "in the process of," rather than accomplished and finished. God did not create the universe once, long ago, but is constantly in the act of creating. God did not save once, on the first Good Friday two thousand years ago, but is always drawing us toward wholeness and well-being.

Process theology, which like "death of God" theology emerged as a response to traditional and increasingly discredited ways of thinking about God, centers around this notion of the divine unfolding. In place of the idea that God created the world according to a plan that is now being followed, with slight deviations made if God is petitioned with sufficient humility and faith, process theology sees God in a fluid, evolving, creative process that constantly interacts with creation. God does not command or will things into being but lures, persuades, attracts, loves. God's absoluteness does not lie in God's omnipotence, omniscience, or immutability, but in the fact that God *always* loves, is always present, is always creating and recreating. Thus, God in process thought is described as the cosmic thrust toward good, the Ground of our Being, a subtle pressure, primordial being. God is always "disclosing Love's absolute meaning for the world, suffering in the life of the world, and rejoicing in creative human growth."[17]

Feminists recognize God as *Sophia* or *Ruach*—God as the cosmic Wisdom that breathes life and goodness into the world and into human lives, as unfailing and pervasive as the air that sustains our physical bodies; God laboring to birth newness and beauty; God "irresistible, beneficent, humane," pervading and penetrating all things (Wis 7:22b–23a, 24b); God as Spirit interceding for us (Rom 8:26) and blowing where [she] wills (John 3:8).

In his massive study of the archetype of the Great Mother in human religion and psychology, Erich Neumann describes Sophia in the Judeo-Christian literature as the symbol of transformation and spiritual unfolding: "This feminine-maternal wisdom is no abstract, disinterested knowledge, but a wisdom of loving participation. . . . Sophia is living and present and near, a godhead that can always be summoned . . . not a deity living inaccessible to man in numinous seclusion."[18] Sophia-Spirit is not the Other, distinct from or alien to creation, but is the All in All, suffusing everything, linking and sanctifying everything. She is like the depths of the sea, undergirding and holding together the crashing turbulence of our lives. The power of

Sophia-Spirit is not the authoritative power exerted over another, but is the indefatigable power of love to attract and transform. Like the ancient Goddess worshiped in the form of the cosmic egg or universal womb, Sophia-Spirit is Matrix, "beneath and around us as encompassing source of life and renewal of life."[19]

In this light, the metaphor of the "hand of God" is changed from a manipulative, interventionist image to a cradling one. Rather than the "hand of God" being referred to in order to describe sudden and often cataclysmic events, it becomes the picture of a gentle, sustaining presence. Julian of Norwich described a vision in which she saw the universe as a little hazelnut, resting in the palm of God's hand, and she marveled at the tenderness of God's love for our fragility.

Several years after I had read and been moved by that vision, my mother was dying of cancer. She told me how disturbed she was that for the first time in her life she found that she could not pray. Her faith in "the Almighty"—the name she used for God—was not broken, but her spiritual life, like her physical body, had been racked by the disease, and she could no longer summon up the energy or focus to pray. My response, after several days spent pondering this, was to send her a card from Julian's hermitage in Norwich that depicted a child resting in the palm of God's hand. Active prayer gives way to the prayer of being in God's presence. The God to whom we cry for help is the God who never left us, and never will.

Fear, Doubt, and Growing Up

To critics of feminist theology this understanding of God is insufficient. Donald Bloesch's book *Is the Bible Sexist?* is an explicit defense of a patriarchal form of Christian thinking, and he insists that prayer must be "bowing down before God and pleading for his mercy and favour."[20] To image God as loving creation to fulfillment while being immersed in it, not separate from it, is, he says, utterly at odds with the biblical image of God initiating creation and redemption, intervening in history, and imposing his will upon his people. In a breathtakingly alarmist summary of the dangers of feminist thought, Bloesch writes:

> I believe that the language of patriarchy was adopted by the Spirit of God in his writing of Holy Scripture because there is an abiding truth in patriarchy that cannot be lightly dismissed. Patriarchy preserves the biblical principle of an above and a below, of a first and a second, of headship and servanthood. To deny or erase these distinctions . . . is to end up in a pantheistic monism in which creaturehood is swallowed up in deity. It is also to end in a social egalitarianism where children have equal voice with parents. . . . It is to open the door to all kinds of sexual promiscuity and perversion. . . . It means the end of the family . . . an all-powerful state . . . government-financed abortion clinics.[21]

Clearly there is not only theological opposition here but also tremendous fear—and not least fear of God, who might "swallow up" the created one. The longed for union with God expressed by the mystics is somehow the object of terror for one whose God is superior, dominating, totally Other. Fear of God is then a virtue, for God is capable of terrifying deeds. The ancient catechism of the church asks, "What is your duty towards God?" And the correct answer begins, "To believe in him, to fear him, and to love him."[22] Fear as an impetus for belief has been used unashamedly in Christian missionary activity for centuries, whether fear of hell-fire, fear of the missionaries who were socially and culturally more powerful than the "heathen," or fear of a system that enforced belief and used capital punishment for dissenters.

Fear continues to be used today, in more or less subtle ways, to discourage religious thought that differs from the mainstream. As a teenager asking religious questions I was told by my conservative evangelical Christian friends that my faith would completely collapse if I questioned any part of it. I wanted to have faith, so I became afraid to doubt. I was also told that I could not trust my own experience or think things out for myself, because my fallen human nature was such that, left to itself, it would inevitably drift away from God under the influence of the devil. Moreover, if I questioned what was in the Bible I was in danger of idolatry—creating a God in my own image rather than believing in the God revealed in Holy Scripture. In Sunday school I was taught verses that were seen as proof of the Bible's inerrant truth:

> All scripture is inspired by God and is useful for teaching, for reproof, for correction, and for training in righteousness. (2 Tim 3:16)

> I warn everyone who hears the words of the prophecy of this book: if anyone adds to them, God will add to that person the plagues described in this book; if anyone takes away from the words of the book of this prophecy, God will take away that person's share in the tree of life and in the holy city. (Rev 22:18–19)

One had constantly to be on the lookout for the devil and his wiles, for he was like a lion prowling about, seeking prey (1 Pet 5:8).

The liberal churches I attended as a young adult were too sophisticated to take the devil literally, but the fear of God continued to be a theme underlying much of the liturgy, with prayers beseeching God to be merciful punctuating the praise and petitions. Doubt was more acceptable, but the fear lay not in becoming fodder for the devil so much as in becoming "merely" a humanist, rationalist, or atheist. There was also the fear of isolation; the communal dimension of faith is important and, at best, sustaining, but it can become a control mechanism when the community member at the margins fears rejection or is threatened with ejection. Many churchgoers simply do not voice their doubts, for fear that they will be perceived as no longer belonging and asked to leave. It was fear of having to resign my ministry and leave the church that made my crisis of faith as a young deaconess assume such painful enormity.

Perhaps one of the most radical gifts of feminism, then, is its affirmation that our lived experience is to be trusted. Our stories, doubts, convictions, and changes are all part of the process of discovering God. Our lack of belief, our times of experiencing the death of our image of God, can be entries into transformed faith. I have always been moved by a prayer from the Iona community in Scotland that upholds "those who need to forget the God they do not believe in and meet the God who believes in them."[23] We sometimes need permission to stop believing.

Feminist theologian Sheila Collins states: "If theology is to be meaningful for us, it must not start with abstractions, but with *our stories*—just as the early Hebrews and Christians of the Bible began with theirs. . . . The process of discovering and naming God is the process of our own liberation or salvation."[24] For the entirety of Christian history and for many centuries before that, women's stories and experience have not been told or trusted. Not one book in the Bible is credited to a female author. Not one of the women who followed Jesus has been recognized by the church as a disciple. When the women ran from the empty tomb to tell the male disciples that Christ was risen, the disciples dismissed their report as nonsense (Luke 24:11).

As for women's physical experiences, the female processes of menstruation, pregnancy, childbirth, and lactation have been named as defiling, part of woman's curse. That they might be used as metaphors for God's love and nurturing of us is regarded with distaste. And so half of humanity in the Judeo-Christian tradition has been excluded from the sacred tasks of imaging God, developing ritual, writing theology, and leading worship, and religion presents an unbalanced picture of God that, for men as well as women, is ultimately unwhole and unholy.

To tell our stories, to explore our doubts, to trust our experience, is to risk. We risk being wrong or being thought wrong, we risk standing alone, and we risk launching out on a journey with no map. The certainty of infallible dogma is attractive, as the current popularity of fundamentalism demonstrates. But when intellectual integrity is sacrificed on the altar of certainty, an idol has been created. For many, the idol has been an all-powerful father God who saves believers from the painful realities of loss, doubt, weakness, or risk. An infantile dependency is encouraged, with church leaders in a parental role and congregants largely passive recipients of "the faith." Of this idol Sallie McFague writes:

> Any notion of salvation which presumes that individuals can be rescued *from* the world; that does not take seriously our necessary efforts to participate in the struggle against oppression and for well-being; or that allows us to abjure our

responsibility by appealing as children to a father who will alone protect and save—any such notion must be seen as immoral, irrelevant, and destructive. At the very least, it cannot be a model for adults; moreover, it is, I believe, contrary to Christian faith.[25]

Growing up is necessary. In order to integrate our lives in all their complexity, and pain with our faith, we have to put away what Pittenger calls "childish notions of divine intrusions and rescue expeditions" and discover the ever present God who is in relationship but not in control.

McFague puts forward the image of God as friend as an alternative that takes seriously the insights of feminism and process thought. The image presupposes that we are not puppets whom God controls or predestines according to a fixed plan, nor are we helpless children; rather, we are adults cocreating, cooperating with God. We are in relationship with a God who is the source of our lives but is also alongside us—transcendent *and* immanent. The emphasis here is not on the awe, wonder, and otherness of God (aspects which have been overemphasized in Christian theology), but on God's presence with us. God as friend, partner, and companion works with us for our salvation, and is faithful, loving, and compassionate. We in turn grow into the realization that we are free to cooperate with God or not, free to share with God our suffering, our joy, our very selves. Through relationship, which includes the honest communication of our thoughts and concerns that we call prayer, the heart is, as Julian of Norwich put it, "oned" with God.

McFague concludes her reflections on God as friend with the reminder that no single model is adequate. Models of transcendence must be complemented by models of immanence; images from human experience by images from nature. Often it is when one model breaks down that the work of finding a new and meaningful one begins. This is the painful process of doubt.

When I collided with doubt early in my ministry as a deaconess, tragedy undermining theology, it felt like the end. It was a loss of innocence, a loss of the ability to package life and death neatly according to my theology. The meaningless death of a young woman broke through the hull of my faith like an iceberg. But it was a necessary collision. Loss of faith is the vital serpentine shedding of old, inadequate images of God. We stand shaken and bereft at the graveside of faith, while the Spirit calls us to follow her into a deeper wisdom.

> Do not remember the former things,
> or consider the things of old.
> I am about to do a new thing;
> now it springs forth, do you not perceive it? (Isa 43:18–19)

Notes

1. J. Mitchell, "Introduction," in *The God I Want* (ed. Mitchell; London: Constable, 1967), 21–22.

2. Elisabeth Moltmann-Wendel and Jurgen Moltmann, "Becoming Human in New Community," in *The Community of Women and Men in the Church* (ed. Constance Parvey; Geneva: World Council of Churches, 1983), 29.

3. William Hamilton, "The New Essence of Christianity" in *Toward a New Christianity* (ed. Thomas J. J. Altizer; New York: Harcourt, Brace and World, 1967), 269.

4. Friedrich Nietzsche, *Thus Spake Zarathustra* (trans. Thomas Common; New York: Prometheus Books, 1993), 276.

5. One such author was Robert Farrer Capon, in his *The Third Peacock* (Garden City, NY: Doubleday, 1971).

6. Quoted in Elisabeth Moltmann-Wendel and Jürgen Moltmann, *Humanity in God* (London: SCM Press, 1983), 60.

7. Frances Young, *Can These Dry Bones Live?* (London: SCM Press, 1982), 57.

8. Hamilton, "Essense of Christianity," 282.

9. William Miller, in Mitchell, *God I Want*, 54.

10. Norman Pittenger, *The Lure of Divine Love* (New York: Pilgrim, 1979), 114, 116.

11. Mary Daly, *Beyond God the Father* (Boston: Beacon, 1973), 71.

12. Sue Woodroff, *Meditations with Mechtild of Magdeburg* (Sante Fe, N.M.: Bear and Co., 1982), 46.

13. Gabriel Uhlein, ed., *Meditations with Hildegard of Bingen* (Sante Fe, N.M.: Bear and Co., 1982), 30, 31.

14. Quoted in Matthew Fox, *The Coming of the Cosmic Christ* (San Francisco: HarperSanFrancisco, 1988), 124.

15. Quoted in Fox, *Coming of the Cosmic Christ*, 115, 116.

16. The Book of Common Prayer (Toronto: Anglican Book Centre, 1962), 528.

17. James B. Nelson, *Embodiment* (Minneapolis: Augsburg, 1978), 245.

18. Erich Neumann, *The Great Mother* (trans. Ralph Manheim; Princeton, N.J.: Bollingen, 1974), 330–31.

19. Rosemary Radford Ruether, *Sexism and God-Talk* (London: SCM Press, 1983), 49.

20. Donald G. Bloesch, *Is the Bible Sexist?* (Westchester, Ill.: Crossway Books, 1982), 64.

21. Ibid., 79.

22. Book of Common Prayer, 548.

23. *The Wee Worship Book* (Glasgow: Wild Goose Worship Group, 1989), 29.

24. Sheila Collins, "Theology in the Politics of Appalachian Women," in *Womanspirit Rising* (ed. Carol P. Christ and Judith Plaskow; San Francisco: Harper Collins, 1992), 151, 155.

25. Sallie McFague, *Metaphorical Theology* (London: SCM Press, 1983), 185–86.

CHAPTER 4
Freedom: Sin, Salvation, and Liberation

IN 1982, ONE YEAR AFTER MY HUSBAND DAVID had been ordained deacon in the Church of England and I had been "made" deaconess (the word "ordained" was studiously avoided, since a deaconess was not considered to be in holy orders), David was ordained priest. It was almost automatic. A deacon was seen as an apprentice, learning from an experienced priest in ministry and graduating after a year to full priesthood if all went well. We had been in university, theological college, and ministry together, studying and working as equals, but now I could go no further. The night before the ordination a group of us gathered to keep vigil, men and women who were working and praying for the ordination of women. We sang and prayed quietly together, then hugged each other at the end. Some of us wept, others raged, at the injustice of women's exclusion from the life of the church. Many, like me, were deaconesses. Some had been in ministry for almost fifty years and were still waiting, working, hoping. Others were men like David, ordained but unable to keep silent about the exclusion of their female colleagues and friends who shared a vocation to the priesthood. I was generously supported but felt very alone.

Anger in women often turns back on itself into depression. We know how to be nice but not angry. We fear the labels that name us shrill, frustrated, bitter, extreme. We are told that we will cause scandal, split the church, jeopardize ecumenical relations, disturb the faithful. So we learn to bite our tongues and go slowly, carefully. We become experts at being sensitive to others' feelings, and we learn diplomacy, charm, how not to seem threatening. And slowly but surely our spirit dies.

In 1975 the General Synod of the Church of England had resolved that there were no theological objections to the ordination of women, but had decided to do nothing at that time.[1] The situation had continued in a stalemate through my years in university, theological college, and parish work. I continued in ministry with David and a senior priest-mentor, both of whom affirmed my gifts and stretched the rules as far as possible to include me, but I felt increasingly discouraged and hopeless. As the fruitless debate about the ordination of women went on and on, and as colleagues and parishioners who stood opposed assured me that they were not personally hostile to me and urged me not to take it to heart so much, my sense of vocation faltered and I began to question whether I could continue. Mary Daly has rightly said that the work of ridding religion of sexism requires "an extraordinary degree of creative rage, love, and hope,"[2] and I was running out of all three. In their place a tired cynicism was growing, both toward the Bible, which was being used as a tool to negate women's gifts, and toward the church, which, having initially been a place where I felt nurtured and affirmed, was now the mouthpiece repeatedly uttering its No to me. I was dismayed and hurt, too, by friends and spiritual mentors or role models who admitted that they were opposed to women's ordination. My vocation was becoming a burden that I was tempted to guard as a secret in order to protect myself from disapproval.

It was David who suggested we leave England and work in a part of the Anglican Communion where women could be ordained. Our focus shifted, and instead of staying and working for as long as it took to bring about change, we began to explore ways to escape. It felt a little disloyal, this plan to leap over the wall, but it also felt like an enormous adventure, and it revived my hope. When my sisters in ministry, the women without the luxury of leaving, gave me their blessing, I knew I was free. In the summer of 1984 we immigrated to Canada, and the following spring I was ordained priest.

The Anglican Church of Canada had been ordaining women for several years, so the fundamental step forward had been taken. Some individuals and some parishes still opposed the development, but the official climate in the denomination was accepting of women as priests, and affirming of our gifts. As women priests became less novel and the fruits of women's ministry emerged, so the resistance began to soften. At my first Eucharist as priest a colleague from a neighboring parish preached, and he confessed that not long before he had been an opponent to the ordination of women. I was moved and surprised when he said that it was through knowing me and other ordained women like me that he had changed his mind. By comparison to the sense of stagnation in the Church of England over women priests, there was excitement and at times euphoria in the Canadian church.

A cautionary note was sounded for me a few weeks before my ordination when I went to hear Mary Daly speak at McGill University in Montreal. A post-Christian by then, Daly gave a blistering presentation on feminism and theology and refused to take questions from men in the audience, on the grounds that historically men had silenced the voices of women, and it was necessary to redress the balance. Invited to meet her at a reception following the lecture, I approached her rather timidly and asked how, as a woman about to be ordained into the church, I could change it from within to become a less sexist organization. She replied that the task was impossible, and compared it to a person of color wanting to join the Ku Klux Klan to make it less racist. This was not encouraging! But then she gave me a hug and wished me well. I understood that I was free to make my own journey and deal with the obstacles I encountered along the way according to my own wisdom and discernment.

Liberation Theology

There are aspects of women's struggle for ordination and of my own experiences in that process that are akin to the process described by liberation theology, which began to emerge from Latin America in the 1960s.[3] Liberation theology identifies freedom as the central theme of the gospel: freedom from oppression, slavery, prejudice, poverty, exile, suffering. And the quest of women in the church to find our place and our voice, and to see in God a face we recognize, is part of a global struggle for liberation and justice.

A fundamental text for liberation theology is a prophecy from Isaiah that Jesus applied to himself at the start of his ministry:

> The spirit of the Lord GOD is upon me,
> because the LORD has anointed me;
> he has sent me to bring good news to the oppressed,
> to bind up the brokenhearted,
> to proclaim liberty to the captives,
> and release to the prisoners;
> to proclaim the year of the LORD's favor. (Isa 61:1–2; cf. Luke 4:18–19)

God is seen as taking sides not with the rich and powerful, despite their claims to be divinely sanctioned, but with the powerless, the marginalized, those whose voice is not heard. Liberation theology speaks of God, for example, as having a "preferential option for the poor." Liberation theology is therefore always subversive because it challenges the status quo, which tolerates or creates injustice. It is always passionate, activist, and experiential, emerging from the crucible of lived experience rather than from abstract, dispassionate academic study. It comes from the gut and heart as well as the head, and it requires not just *orthodoxy* (the right way of believing) but also *orthopraxis* (the right way of living). It issues a challenge to believers to "walk the talk," to embody in their lives and politics and society the values they claim to espouse. Liberation theology has a deeply communal dimension, so that salvation is not defined primarily as a personal conversion experience but as a communal *metanoia*, or turning around, away from all that oppresses and toward all that brings freedom.

As people of faith have found their voice, the theology of liberation has been proclaimed by the poor, by homosexuals, by women, by people of color; any to whom the gospel has come as a message of freedom. And their voices have been ringing with anger and recovered pride. They follow a savior who is not robed like an emperor but who has blood and sweat on his face and dirt under his fingernails. Feminist theology embraces liberation theology as foundational; freedom is basic to the gospel.

In the 1970s proponents of the ordination of women were often dismissed as "women's libbers" jumping on a secular bandwagon of equal rights. The movement was frequently caricatured as untheological, as a "worldly" issue that had trespassed onto holy ground. Indeed, the Church of England was exempt from the emerging national legislation prohibiting discrimination in employment on the grounds of gender, because it argued that the issue was a secular one whereas the ordination of men only was an ecclesiastical matter. The understanding was that the rules were different for spiritual matters. Yet feminist theologians have rightly insisted that the treatment of women both inside the church and outside is a profoundly spiritual issue. Mary Daly, for instance, sees the liberation of women to full personhood as a necessary precondition for all forms of human liberation, since it breaks down the fundamental divide, the "original sin" of one human viewing another as innately subordinate. It also frees us from the false god of control and dominating power, to find the God in whose image women can know themselves created: "The becoming of women may be not only the doorway to deliverance from the omnipotent Father in all of his guises . . . but also . . . the beginning for many of a more authentic search for transcendence; that is, for God."[4]

Author Sara Maitland makes the same point and uses the striking image of the church as the pregnant body of Christ, with women bringing to birth a new creation and a new relationship to God:

> The Body of Christ (as Paul does *not* say) is a pregnant body; pregnant with the new birth, the New Creation, pregnant with Salvation. Throughout the Church's history, group after group, and individual after individual from within the Christian community have been called upon to be the midwives to this pregnancy. . . . The demands that women are making of their churches and of the world, for full humanity, is—or can be—the prophetic voice crying in the wilderness for a return to God, to adventure and to hope.[5]

The women's movement has given rise to a feminist theology which proclaims to *all* people the good news of liberation and becoming.

Sin and Salvation

From a liberationist perspective the gospel has a communal, even cosmic, dimension. Sin is defined as something far more complex than "doing wrong" within a moralistic or legalistic framework. Salvation, as the remedy for sin, is understood in a different light, with the focus not on forgiveness so much as on freedom. It is helpful to consider the commonly held or popular understandings of sin and salvation, especially as they have entered into religious and cultural thought today, before moving on to the contributions of feminist and liberationist thought.

Sin as Breaking God's Laws

At its most basic level, sin is traditionally seen as the committing of an offense against God's commandments. From the book of Genesis, where Adam and Eve are portrayed as breaking the very first divine command not to eat the fruit of the forbidden tree, through the listing of the Ten Commandments in Exod 20 and the several hundred laws in the five "books of Moses," to the book of Revelation with its graphic and violent description of the punishments awaiting those who do not obey God's commandments, God is the lawgiver and sinners are those who break the law. Although there are certainly biblical texts that contextualize these laws societally and relationally, the primary setting is a legalistic one: These are God's rules; obey them.

In keeping with this, confession is a matter of listing the sins one has committed. In a congregational setting, the listing is generalized, such as in this prayer from the Book of Common Prayer's form for evening worship:

> Almighty and most merciful Father, We have erred and strayed from thy ways like lost sheep, We have followed too much the devices and desires of our own hearts, We have offended against thy holy laws, We have left undone those things which we ought to have done, And we have done those things which we ought not to have done; And there is no health in us.

The tone is self-accusing, pessimistic, and takes for granted that "miserable sinners" stand in need of pleading for God's mercy much as a convict in a court of law would plead for clemency from the judge. It also conveys the idea that the human heart cannot be trusted; there is a deep distrust of our humanness as flawed and weak, "our own hearts" as devious and selfish.

For personal confessions, to be made in the presence of a priest, inventories of sins are drawn up for the penitent to go through as a checklist of possible offenses. Cultural and religious attitudes are sometimes humorously evident in these lists. As theological students we were amused to find one inventory designed for members of a male monastic order which, alongside fornication and impure thoughts, listed

"Going on retreat for the food" as a potential sin for which the monk should search his conscience.

There are benefits to this approach to sin and confession. As a pious young Anglo-Catholic, the regular experience of making my confession to a priest and hearing his advice and absolution was cathartic. The exercise of searching my heart and memory for ways in which I had fallen short encouraged a certain honesty and self-knowledge. But this is only a small step away from a form of ritualistic legalism that creates self-satisfaction, hypocrisy, and false purity. The Protestant's caricature of the Catholic going to confession every week, receiving absolution, and then going straight out to commit the same sins is a response to this. So too was Jesus' piercing denunciation of the Pharisees who regarded themselves as ritually pure because they observed the required codes of holiness but who treated the poor and outcast with contempt (see, e.g., Matt 15:1–9; 23:1–28).

Sin as breaking God's rules does not go far enough. It fosters a childish understanding of righteousness as "being good," and it slides easily into the legalism of external purity rather than internal attitude. It is also liable to make the rules of the powerful the laws of God, so that the challenging of social or political structures is interpreted as defying God and punished accordingly. The religious authorities define and mediate God's commandments, and dissidents become blasphemers. Thus, during the Cold War Americans saw communists as evil atheists, since they challenged the (God-given) rules of capitalism. And in Afghanistan, under the fundamentalist rule of the Taliban, women who broke the laws that confined them to subservience and invisibility were punished harshly as enemies of God.

Feminists are often accused of breaking God's laws that specify correct relationships between the sexes. When I was ordained a priest I knew that in the eyes of some I was contravening the regulations laid down for the early Christian community as found in the New Testament, whereby women were not to be in authority over men, even as teachers, but were to listen and learn quietly and submissively (see 1 Cor 14:34–35 and 1 Tim 2:11–12). Going by the book, especially when the book is uncritically read as containing God's very words, means maintaining the status quo. This cannot be good news for those seeking liberation from it.

Sin as Separation from God

A less law-centered understanding of sin sees it as that which comes between us and God, or that which leads us away from God. Sinners are described as being far from God, rebellious, or proud, and repentance means returning to God. So the prophet Hosea urges Israel:

> Return, O Israel, to the LORD your God,
>   for you have stumbled because of your iniquity.
> Take words with you

> and return to the LORD;
> say to him,
>   "Take away all guilt"; . . .

> They shall again live beneath my shadow. (Hos 14:1–2, 7)

Sin is as much a question of the heart's disposition as the deeds done. It is forgetting
God or being unfaithful to God. The analogy of marital infidelity is used by Hosea
to describe this breaking not of rules but of covenant love:

> For now, O Ephraim, you have played the whore;
>   Israel is defiled.
> Their deeds do not permit them
>   to return to their God.
> For the spirit of whoredom is within them,
>   and they do not know the LORD. (Hos 5:3–4)

This is Paul's understanding of sin, when he writes of the way in which it alien-
ates humanity from God and results in ever more degrading guilt:

> For though they knew God, they did not honor him as God or give thanks to
> him, but they became futile in their thinking, and their senseless minds were
> darkened. Claiming to be wise, they became fools. . . . Therefore God gave
> them up in the lusts of their hearts to impurity, to the degrading of their bodies
> among themselves, because they exchanged the truth about God for a lie. (Rom
> 1:21–22, 24–25)

The deadliest sin is often identified as pride, the self-glorying arrogance of
humanity that sees no need of God or refuses to walk in God's ways. Pride is
described as foolish, wicked, and deceptive,[6] and its remedy is humility, submission,
and obedience to God. The proud must be brought low.[7] The language is that of
hierarchy, the image is of a struggle for power. Coercion, threats, and punishments
are used in the attempt to establish or prove God's ultimate supremacy:

> If you will not obey me, and do not observe all these commandments, . . . I will
> bring terror on you. . . . I will set my face against you. . . . I will continue to
> punish you sevenfold for your sins. I will break your proud glory. . . . You shall
> eat the flesh of your sons, and you shall eat the flesh of your daughters. . . . I will
> heap your carcasses on the carcasses of your idols. . . . I will unsheathe the sword
> against you. . . . You shall perish. (Lev 26:14ff.)

Feminists and others have rightly critiqued this conflictual, retributive image of God. It makes God simply the most powerful male, before whom all must ultimately bow not out of love but submission. Armageddon is this God's final weapon, the global destruction of the wicked. It comes as no surprise that it was a country which claims to follow this God that launched the first nuclear attack on a political enemy and precipitated a Cold War that saw the earth bristling with enough nuclear weapons to bring about the end of all human and other forms of life.

Sin as Failure to Return God's Love

In total contrast to a doctrine of sin that results in a macho, intolerant God, sin can be seen as a tragic failure of the creature to return the Creator's love. The consequent evil, alienation, and suffering that follow are not punishments but the natural outcome of this failure. God is not vengeful but grief stricken. In her exploration of the nature of God as the source of all life, energy, and love, Rosemary Haughton writes that God's relationship with creation is one of passionate exchange.[8] It is a dynamic flow back and forth between Creator and creature, but the mutuality breaks down when there is resistance to this process of giving, receiving, and breaking through to newness. The result is tragedy—love refused. Sin is thus not the breaking of a divine law, which requires punishment, so much as the breaking of a relationship, which results in loss.

In Pittenger's description of sin as understood by process theology, he writes that sin is not a contravention of laws imposed from outside by an authoritarian God, but is "a violation of the solicitation and lure of love."[9] Love is God's nature and God's invitation to us to respond. Fear and overpowering force are not factors at play in our relationship with divine love when we understand it rightly—which means nonpatriarchally. Love calls us to come to maturity and to express love in the world as we work with God to bring creation to its intended fulfillment. So Pittenger affirms: "Each man and woman is constantly challenged to be a co-creator of good, and a co-worker in good, with the cosmic thrust toward good that religious people name God, thus participating in the enormously demanding effort to overcome evil, injustice, oppression, suffering, and whatever else in creation works against that good."[10]

Biblical texts also speak of God's absolute love and our freedom to respond to it or reject it. Love, according to Paul, is the fulfilling of the law (see Rom 13:10), and the First Epistle of John rests on an understanding of love as primary and definitive of God, with no shadow of the threat of retributive punishment:

> Beloved, let us love one another, because love is from God; everyone who loves is born of God and knows God. Whoever does not love does not know God, for God is love. . . . There is no fear in love, but perfect love casts out fear; for fear

has to do with punishment, and whoever fears has not reached perfection in love. We love because he first loved us. (1 John 4:7–8, 18–19)

Jesus' parable of the Prodigal Son is a story of the unconditional love of God and the divine vulnerability that is wounded when love is refused (Luke 15:11–32).

As feminist thought examines the concept of sin and its various understandings in biblical and Christian traditions, it does so with the knowledge that our definition of sin will reflect our image of God. Is God perceived primarily as lawgiver or as lover? As judge or as healer? Does God mirror the ruling class and its requirements, or is God seen to champion the marginalized? Is a softer image of a God who does not mete out punishment a product of wishful thinking, or an intentional departure from the brutal images of patriarchy? Fundamental questions such as these affect the entire edifice of theology that we subsequently build and assume to be self-evident.

Women's Sin

Of particular relevance to us here is the definition of sin as manifested in women, or as critiqued by feminism. Patriarchy's view of sin as a resistance to the power of God through pride either does not consider women capable of such sin (because of their relative weakness), or unthinkingly assumes that the sin of pride is the sin of all humanity. When it considers female sin specifically, it is usually equated with sexuality. Thus, Eve is not just the first to sin but is a seductive, sexual temptress. Prostitution and harlotry are common accusations against biblical women who are considered sinful:

What peace can there be, so long as the many whoredoms and sorceries of your mother Jezebel continue? (2 Kgs 9:22)

In those days . . . a certain Levite . . . took to himself a concubine from Bethlehem in Judah. But his concubine prostituted herself against him and she went away from him. (Judg 19:1–2)

Then one of the seven angels who had the seven bowls came and said to me, "Come, I will show you the judgment of the great whore who is seated on many waters" . . . and I saw a woman . . . clothed in purple and scarlet, and adorned with gold and jewels and pearls, holding in her hand a golden cup full of abominations and the impurities of her fornication; and on her forehead was written a name, a mystery: "Babylon the great, mother of whores and of earth's abominations." And I saw that the woman was drunk with the blood of the saints and the blood of the witnesses to Jesus. (Rev 17:1, 3–6)

Whether the language is historical or metaphorical, the association of women with sexual sin is clear. In addition, the woman in Luke 7:36–50 who washes Jesus' feet with her tears, dries them with her hair, and kisses and anoints them is described as "a sinner," and the assumption of sexual sin (following this highly sensual act) is clear when Jesus' host says to himself, "If this man were a prophet, he would have known who and what kind of woman this is who is touching him—that she is a sinner" (Luke 7:39).

Similarly, Mary Magdalene, from whom Jesus is said to have cast out seven demons (Luke 8:2), has become in popular legend the supreme example of the penitent prostitute, as her brokenness has long been equated with sexual sin. She is often, in fact, a composite and completely unhistorical figure when she is portrayed as an amalgamation of the unnamed woman in Luke 7, Mary of Bethany in John 12, and the disciple Mary Magdalene. Of her sexualized and mangled story Elisabeth Moltmann-Wendel writes: "A two thousand year old history of male fantasies has painted over and distorted the original story. This compares only with the process in which the matriarchal goddesses were patriarchalized and changed from universality to sexual roles."[11]

Because of the association of women's sin with sexual sin, and the links between sexual sin and religious "idolatry" in the form of worship of the Goddess, women's sexuality was severely repressed and denigrated, and a woman's submission to her husband or father was required. It was considered sinful for a woman to decorate her hair or wear jewelry; she was to wear a head covering as a symbol of submission; humility, meekness, obedience, and servanthood were to be her virtues (see 1 Tim 2:9–15; 1 Cor 11:5–15). When she stood up for herself and refused to be treated as property, she was guilty of insubordination; when she was meek and subservient, she was regarded as morally weak and easily misguided.

The Judeo-Christian legacy for women has been a strong sense of self-doubt. When the norm is masculine control absolutized in a Father God, and when divine images of female power are absent, women have no mirror in which to see their strength, beauty, and selfhood. The result is self-negation, what Carol Christ calls "a uniquely female form of sin."[12] In a significant article in 1960 Valerie Saiving Goldstein wrote:

> The temptations of woman as woman are not the same as the temptations of man as man, and the specifically feminine forms of sin . . . have a quality which can never be encompassed by such terms as "pride" and "will to power." They are better suggested by such terms as triviality, distractibility, and diffuseness; lack of an organizing center or focus, dependence on others for one's self-definition; tolerance at the expense of standards of excellence. . . . In short, under-development or negation of the self.[13]

Saiving's contention is not that all women are by nature trivial and underdeveloped as persons, but that patriarchal religion and culture have created a climate in which such traits tend to result. Like a plant deprived of light, whose growth is pale and straggly not because that is its nature but because it has not been given conditions in which it can flourish, women can fall prey to a passivity, an uncreativity, a failure to actualize our gifts and potential as a result of our socialization to be the weaker or gentler sex. Women may attempt to follow the commandments to love God and neighbor, but often fail even to notice the injunction that we are to love our neighbor *as we love ourselves* (Matt 22:37–39; Mark 12:29–31; Luke 10:27). Lack of self-love may be our primary "sin."

Feminist theologian Judith Plaskow maintains that the traditional centrality of pride as sin comes from a narrow masculine perspective that entirely fails to take into account women's experience. Grace thus becomes linked with humbling oneself to the will of another—namely, God—but this is precisely the predicament or sin of women. As Simone de Beauvoir wrote half a century ago:

> What particularly signalizes the situation of woman is that she—a free autonomous being like all human creatures—nevertheless finds herself living in a world where men compel her to assume the status of the Other. They propose to stabilize her as an object and to doom her to immanence since her transcendence is to be overshadowed and forever transcended by another ego which is essential and sovereign.[14]

Plaskow concludes that we must turn upside down the old notions of sin, self-sacrifice, and salvation. Sin when defined as pride, as a usurping of the place of God, as a willful breaking of God's laws, as self-assertion, is not typical of women's sin. The opposite is true: Women are socialized to hold back, to negate the self, to look to others for direction and fulfillment. And the religious ideals of self-sacrifice, self-denial, and self-giving make a woman's attempts to find and express herself a sin. How many times have women heard that the feminist movement is dangerous and unchristian because it encourages women to depart from their divinely ordained roles as wives and mothers and to challenge their menfolk as head of the house? Yet the acceptance of those roles may be the greater sin because it stifles growth into full personhood.

To express it at its simplest, sin may be not a question of going too far, but of not going far enough. When a human being, male or female, lives a cautious half-life of self-doubt, dependency, and refusal to risk, God's image is obscured and personhood is stunted. The flow of divine love from Creator to created in dynamic interplay becomes blocked. The gift of life is cheapened. It is from this, as well as from our willful turning away from God, that we need to be liberated.

I have a clear memory from the early days of my relationship with David. Looking back at it now I see it as an awakening to my own passivity and self-doubt, and a challenge to hold my ground. We were both undergraduates, theoretically equals. Immersed in our study of theology, discussions and differences of opinion often came up. David was a skilled debater and loved to argue, whereas I shrank from anything that felt like conflict, and usually gave in to his relentless logic. But on this occasion, having once again argued me into silence, David burst out in frustration, "Why do you always let me win? I know you don't agree with me, so why don't you hold your ground?" From that moment I changed; I found some solid ground under my feet and knew I had a right to stand on it. Unbeknownst to David, I suspect, he had given me a gift of liberation.

Models of Salvation

If sin is to be redefined, so too must salvation. Those who have been denied freedom, dignity, and self-esteem need to hear words of liberation. But the classical message of salvation speaks of humans as fallen and wretched, soiled with guilt and in need of rescue. In the model that understands sin to be the breaking of God's commandments, the remedy is as legalistic as the problem: Either the offender must be punished, or the lawmaker and judge may declare clemency. Although expressed in a variety of ways, each of these atonement theologies works with the assumption that sin must in some way be dealt with if we are to be in a right relationship with God. Each also understands the death of Jesus as fundamental to the process of salvation.

One view draws on the Hebraic practice of making sacrifices for sin. Just as the Hebrew Scriptures specified the sacrifices required as offerings for sin, so Jesus was seen as the only fitting sacrifice to atone for humanity's sin. And like the sacrificial animals, he had to die in order to satisfy God's righteous wrath. So Paul wrote to the Romans: "For while we were still weak, at the right time Christ died for the ungodly. . . . Much more surely then, now that we have been justified by his blood, will we be saved through him from the wrath of God" (Rom 5:6, 9).

A variant explanation, but still within the model of the legal system and its requirements, is that in place of humanity God allowed Jesus to suffer the penalty of our sins. Jesus took upon himself the weight of all the sins of the world, and on the cross the death penalty was carried out. Echoing the Hebraic practice of transferring sins onto a "scapegoat" (see Lev 16:20–22) that was set free to roam in the wilderness until it met its death, Jesus was the innocent victim who was substituted for the real offenders: "For our sake [God] made [Jesus] to be sin who knew no sin, so that in him we might become the righteousness of God" (2 Cor 5:21). This substitution of Jesus for us is seen as evidence of God's great mercy and love, although it is only those who are "in Christ"—that is, those who identify themselves as sinners and claim the benefits of Christ's atoning death while bowing to him as Lord—who are thus absolved. God's forgiveness is limited by the bounds of justice, and is conditional upon our repentance. The "ifs" are clear:

> If we confess our sins, he who is faithful and just will forgive us our sins and cleanse us from all unrighteousness. (1 John 1:9)

> If you confess with your lips that Jesus is Lord and believe in your heart that God raised him from the dead, you will be saved. (Rom 10:9)

Forgiveness as God's act solely through Jesus for our salvation is defined succinctly by Peter in the account of his speech before the assembly of Jewish religious leaders in Jerusalem: "There is salvation in no one else, for there is no other name under heaven given among mortals by which we must be saved" (Acts 4:12).

The language of ransom or redemption is also used with reference to God's deliverance of us from sin. Implicit in the concept of ransom is that the enemy who captured us (the devil) is paid off with the offering of Christ's life as the price (see, e.g., Matt 20:28 and Rev 5:9). Again, the image is that of a transaction between parties, with humanity as the passive recipient of salvation.

Herein lies the problem with atonement theologies of this kind. Whether defined as an appeasing sacrifice, a penal substitution, or a ransom, the redeeming act of God in Christ permits no cooperation on the part of humanity. We are sinners, totally dependent on God's grace. "There is no health in us," mourns an ancient prayer of confession.[15] Sallie McFague's critique of this, as she proposes the alternative model of God as friend, is that it can have pernicious results:

> It projects an image of human life as infantile, individualistic, and isolated. It has tended to stress an all-powerful father of helpless children, some of whom, as favored, are rescued individually from a sinful world. . . . It is deeply in need of substantial revision, for human life cannot responsibly be seen in those terms. Nor . . . does Jesus as parable of God, either in his teaching or his activity, support such a view.[16]

In contrast to the legalistic understanding of God and salvation, which became normative in Christian theology, other models are being explored that do not cast humanity in the role of condemned convict or imprisoned hostage, nor rely on images of God as divine executioner or rescuer.

Salvation as Healing to Wholeness

Like the prophets who called their people to come back to God, Jesus proclaimed repentance, or turning around, not in the sense of listing sins committed and begging a wrathful God for mercy, but in the deeper sense of reorienting one's life to be in accord with God's ways of love and justice. He was concerned with the heart, not just the deeds, and called for a reinterpretation of righteousness that went far beyond legalism: "You have heard that it was said, 'You shall love your neighbor and hate your enemy.' But I say to you, Love your enemies and pray for those who persecute you, so that you may be children of your Father in heaven. . . . Be perfect, therefore, as your heavenly Father is perfect" (Matt 5:43–45, 48). When Zacchaeus, the corrupt tax collector, was addressed by Jesus, he turned his life around and let go of his slavery to money, declaring that he would give half of his possessions to the poor and would pay back four times over any whom he had defrauded. Jesus responded, "Today salvation has come to this house" (Luke 19:9). The story is one of invitation and response, of challenge and commitment. Similarly, when a rich young man approached Jesus and asked, "Good Teacher, what must I do to inherit eternal life?" Jesus responded initially that he should keep the commandments. But when the man said that he had kept them all since childhood, Jesus challenged him to go one step further and demonstrate with a life of total commitment and discipleship his desire for the kingdom of God (Mark 10:17–22). Eternal life is not the reward of salvation that the righteous receive, but a life lived in radical commitment to God's ways, symbolized by "the kingdom of God." Salvation is a healed relationship.

It is significant that Jesus repeatedly commended people for having faith that enabled them to become well, whole, or saved. He frequently connected physical or emotional healing with spiritual well-being. So to the woman suffering from a chronic hemorrhage who had the courage to break through the religious taboos and come forward to touch Jesus for healing, he said, "Daughter, your faith has made you well" (Luke 8:43–48). And to the woman who washed his feet with her tears as an expression of gratitude for sins forgiven, he said, "Your faith has saved you" (Luke 7:36–50). The same words are spoken to the blind beggar who called out to Jesus for healing (Luke 18:35–43) and to the tenth leper whom Jesus cured (Luke 17:11–19). Salvation, it would seem from this, is a dynamic process that involves not just our participation but our courageous willingness to step forward, to act, to touch, to call, to give thanks.

The word "salvation" derives from the Latin word *salus*, meaning health or wholeness. Salvation as wholeness does not focus narrowly on evil as the problem, but more widely identifies it as brokenness. Thus, human wrongdoing is part of the brokenness, but so too is disease, disaster, or other nonhuman factors that bring pain and ugliness into creation. In the struggle for healing and wholeness we work together with God and all of creation in the labor of salvation. Indeed, were we not to participate in our healing, we could not be made whole.

Salvation for Women

In keeping with the realization that the characteristic sin of women is not pride but self-doubt, and following from the understanding of salvation as a process in which God and creation are mutually engaged, a feminist theology sees self-actualization as a major component of salvation for women. We do not wait or even pray to be passively saved, like a fairytale princess helplessly locked up in a tower or menaced by a dragon. We do not view Jesus as the prince who delivers us. Rather, we step forward and cry out for healing and liberation, and hear Jesus as friend commend us for our faith—faith both in God's enabling power that loves us into being, and in ourselves as God's work of art (see Eph 2:10). Salvation means becoming who we were created to be—unique, free, able to give and receive great love.

Indian scientist and Catholic lay activist Astrid Lobo expresses her understanding of salvation as inner empowerment in this way:

> As a woman it is important for me that I am in God and God is in me. No longer do I see God as a rescuer. I see her more as power and strength within me. . . . I no longer see the victim-rescuer game as healthy, so I have learnt to shed the needless dependence on God. I am increasingly aware of the resources God has given me. I feel strongly the need to develop and create as my response to God's love shown in my creation.[17]

The starting point is the awareness not of radical separation from God but of essential union: "I am in God and God is in me." Salvation is the process of realizing (making real) this truth. Salvation is coming home to what most deeply *is*. Jesus is Savior not because he rescues us, dies for us, or does something else to or for us, but because he reveals the truth that sets us free—the truth that we are beloved daughters and sons of God, made in God's image, called to live as he did in the Spirit's creative power. Jesus described his mission as bringing abundant life (John 10:10).

Women are so accustomed to hearing that God requires obedience and submission, that we are to share humbly and patiently in the sufferings of Jesus, that pride separates us from God, and that the human heart cannot be trusted, it requires a theological judo throw to flip the message over and hear words of real salvation. Some feminists have encouraged women to meditate on the positive aspects of words such as "sex," "self," "pride," "passion," and "power."[18] These words have often had negative connotations in religious life and in women's lives, but they can be a vital part of a woman's spiritual coming alive—her salvation from dependency, self-abnegation, or depression. Thus, sexuality can be celebrated as creative energy and attraction, not feared or repressed as inherently sinful. The self can be accepted and loved with gratitude and respect, instead of being "put to death." Pride and passion can be seen as the strength from within that enables a black South African to look a white man in the eye as an equal, or a mother to fight for custody of her children to protect them from their abusive father. Power becomes "integrity, creativity, courage: the mark of a person who is whole."[19]

Salvation for Christian women is encapsulated in Jesus' words of liberation which, collected together, form a resonant message of affirmation and good news:

> Follow me.
>
> You are the salt of the earth. . . . You are the light of the world.
>
> Ask, and it will be given you; search, and you will find; knock, and the door will be opened for you.
>
> Why do you not judge for yourselves what is right?
>
> Take heart, daughter; your faith has made you well.
>
> Do not be afraid.
>
> Woman, great is your faith!
>
> Your faith has saved you; go in peace.
>
> My mother and my sisters and brothers are those who hear the word of God and do it.
>
> You are worried and distracted by many things; there is need of only one thing.
>
> You know [the Spirit of truth], because [she] abides with you, and [she] will be in you.
>
> I do not call you servants but friends.
>
> I appointed you to go and bear fruit.[20]

Our salvation is our vocation, when we hear ourselves called by name, affirmed, empowered, and entrusted with carrying out the liberative work of Jesus as part of the body of Christ. The scope of this liberation is cosmic. And it is urgently needed.

Liberating Christianity and Culture

We live in an era where the sins of the Christian church are abundantly clear. As its victims have found their voices, the church as the divine vehicle of salvation has been deeply discredited. From child abuse in residential schools to sexual misconduct by prominent evangelists, the church carries a legacy of guilt and shame. And this legacy is directly related to theology. We become like the God we worship. If our God requires death, imposes brutal punishment, intimidates and threatens, it should come as no surprise that those who hold authority in the name of this God do likewise.

"Christianity is an abusive theology that glorifies suffering," write Joanne Carlson Brown and Rebecca Parker, theological educators, in *Christianity, Patriarchy, and Abuse.*[21] They describe the connection between a theology of a God who demands the death of his son, and a society where child abuse, sexism, and oppression are prevalent. "If Christianity is to be liberating for the oppressed, it must liberate itself from this theology," they state.[22] They reject atonement theologies as bloodthirsty and sadistic, and are wary of theologies that emphasize God's suffering with us or for us, because they may lead to the idea that if God suffers, then suffering is good—which results in a masochistic spirituality. Instead, they redefine Christianity as in essence about justice, radical love, and liberation. To be a Christian does not mean to accept a certain atonement theory, but to keep faith with those who challenge injustice, refuse to be victims, and struggle for political, ecclesiastical, and personal liberation.

On the phenomenon of women staying in the church while suffering from its abusive teachings and practices, Parker and Carlson Brown write that such women resemble the battered woman who stays with her abusive partner, believing that the abuser is sorry, does not mean to abuse, will change, needs the woman if he is to change, or provides the only security she knows. To continue to stay in such a relationship, or to stay within an abusive church and theology, "is a sign of the depth of our oppression."[23] They conclude, "The only legitimate reason for women to remain in the church will be if the church were to condemn as anathema the glorification of suffering."[24]

As the ugly truth about oppression and abuse in Christianity is laid bare, we experience an anger and a grief that can seem overwhelming, and that can alienate us from the religious institutions that may at first have nurtured us. It is a necessary part of the journey, for it enables us to step back, to stop being uncritically loyal, and to challenge the "orthodoxy" that defines right belief and points the finger at "heresy." As a result, we stop worshiping a God who deals in sacrifice, punishments, or threats. We do not preach a theology that is death centered or that glorifies suffering and revictimizes the victims. We refuse to treat the Bible as God's every word, implying that it contains only truth, or that no truth is contained in other religious texts or traditions. We recognize that traditional Western theology does not have the copyright on Christianity. We are not intimidated by phrases such as, "as the church has always taught," or "in the unbroken tradition of the church fathers," or even, "as Scripture says."

In order for theology to be truly liberative it must be lived. We must pay attention to our experience and learn to recognize the wisdom of our own voice, individually and communally. Speaking of the task before Asian women theologians, feminist theologian Chung Hyun Kyung writes:

> We . . . must move away from our imposed fear of losing Christian identity, in
> the opinion of the mainline theological circles, and instead risk that we might be

transformed by the religious wisdom of our own people. . . . We have to ask tough questions of the mainline Christian churches and seminaries and also of ourselves. Who *owns* Christianity? Is Christianity unchangeable? What makes Christianity Christian?[25]

In her address to the assembly of the World Council of Churches in Canberra, Australia, in 1991, Chung listed three critical changes that must be made if the life-giving breath of the Holy Spirit is to be able to blow through the world and save our planet from destruction: (1) a turning away from anthropocentrism, which puts humanity (and especially powerful males) at the center of the universe rather than putting life in all its forms at the center; (2) a move from the habit of dualism to the habit of interconnectedness; and (3) a change from death-centeredness to life-centeredness.

Our churches, our sacred texts, and our religious authorities all need this repentance. In this respect, "All have sinned and fall short of the glory of God" (Rom 3:23). Our churches need to confess their sins, cleanse themselves of sexism, and make amends for the crimes against indigenous cultures committed by their missionaries. They must embrace truly inclusive language and liturgies, encouraging the use of diverse images for the Divine, welcoming back the Goddess, Sophia-Spirit, and God as "she," and rejoicing in the full participation of women as leaders, priests, ministers, pastors, bishops, educators, activists, mystics, theologians—as gifted human beings. Our sacred texts must not be sacrosanct and immune from criticism, but seen for what they are—namely, human efforts (exclusively male, in the case of the Bible) to express our partial knowledge of God, complete with all the inconsistencies, mistakes, biases, and agenda of the authors. Where necessary we must cease to read them in the context of worship as "the word of the Lord," and instead wrestle with them in the context of cultural and historical study. Always we must approach them with "a hermeneutic of suspicion," that is, with the realization that they are fallible vessels, not ultimate truth. And we can add to them with texts and unwritten wisdom from other traditions as we seek to live out a habit of interconnectedness rather than dualism.

Hong Kong theologian Kwok Pui-lan rejects what she calls a "mystified" view of the Bible as absolute truth, and she encourages a new way to approach it:

For a long time, such "mystified" doctrine has taken away the power from women, the poor and the powerless, for it helps to sustain the notion that the "divine presence" is located somewhere else and not in ourselves. Today, we must claim back the power to look at the Bible with our own eyes and to stress that divine immanence is within us, not in something sealed off and handed down from almost two thousand years ago.[26]

Feminists are therefore finding the courage and imagination to tap our own depths for wisdom and sacred story. The lost women in the Bible and history are being rediscovered and heard; artists portray Jesus as Christa, the crucified woman, cosmic Sophia; liturgists create rituals for the onset of menstruation, for recovery from miscarriage or abortion, for menopause, or after a hysterectomy[27]; and ministry may now include dance, massage, healing circles, storytelling, justice initiatives, peacemaking workshops, social activism and advocacy.

"After five thousand years of living in a dominator society, it is indeed difficult to imagine a different world," writes Riane Eisler. It is difficult, but not impossible. Liberation theology and feminist faith together envision it, and Eisler herself concludes her book with a powerful image of this different world:

> It will be a world where limitation and fear will no longer be systematically taught us through myths about how inevitably evil and perverse we humans are. . . . [Children] will be taught new myths, epics, and stories in which human beings are good; men are peaceful; and the power of creativity and love . . . is the governing principle. . . . And after the bloody detour of androcratic history, both women and men will at last find out what being human can mean.[28]

Hearing God's Yes

A prayer in the Book of Common Prayer, said by the congregation before receiving Holy Communion, begins, "We do not presume to come to this thy table, trusting in our own righteousness." Known as the Prayer of Humble Access, it expresses the unworthiness of humans to approach the Divine. "We are not worthy," it says, "so much as to gather up the crumbs under thy table." I prayed it for years, with my eyes closed, head down, and "meekly kneeling upon my knees" as the rubric required for such prayers of confession and humility.

One day I became aware that a woman who often sat beside me at church was omitting this prayer. I was curious, and listened the next time. Again, she omitted it. I asked her why she did this, and her reply has stayed with me ever since: "All my life I was told that I'm not worthy," she said, "but I believe finally that God says I am. The gospel for me is that I don't have to grovel under the table for crumbs anymore."

There is a place, of course, for humility in the spiritual life. But sometimes that place becomes a prison and we are bowed down under a false sense of shame. Like the crippled woman in Luke's gospel (13:10–17) who was bent over for years, we need to be restored to wholeness so that we can see the face of Christ and hold our heads high.

Salvation is the liberation of hearing God's Yes to us. With God's Yes ringing in our ears we can stand up straight and run and risk and leap over the walls that contain and restrain. We are less biddable, more unpredictable. We may start to pray with our eyes open and heads up, and we may receive Holy Communion standing, not kneeling, as our bodies reflect what our spirits are coming to know.

My own path to the knowledge of God's Yes began when I summoned up the courage to say, in the face of an ecclesiastical No, that I believed I was called to be a priest. It continued as I joined the movement for women's ordination in England and as I immigrated to Canada. The Yes overwhelmed me when I was ordained in Montreal, with the hands of bishop and priests laid on my head and shoulders in blessing and affirmation as tears poured down my face in joy. And still the Yes calls me on, through self-doubt toward passion, and from the desire to play it safe to the willingness to risk everything.

The way is not easy, and I often forget or fall asleep. Fearfulness can drown out the whisper of the Spirit. Once, while struggling to write this book, I went to my spiritual director in an agony of uncertainty and anxiety about whether I could do it and, if I could, whether I should. Jean listened as patiently and attentively as always, then smiled and said, "Lucy, what God says to you is Yes, Yes, Yes."

Notes

1. In July 1975 the General Synod of the Church of England passed a motion affirming that there are no fundamental theological objections to the ordination of women as priests. In addition, a motion to keep in place the existing barriers against women's ordination was defeated. However, a subsequent motion to remove such barriers was also defeated.

2. Mary Daly, "After the Death of God the Father: Women's Liberation and the Transformation of Christian Consciousness," in *Womanspirit Rising* (ed. Carol P. Christ and Judith Plaskow; San Francisco: Harper Collins, 1992), 62.

3. See, e.g., Leonardo Boff and Clodovis Boff, *Introducing Liberation Theology* (Maryknoll, N.Y.: Orbis, 1987).

4. Daly, "After the Death of God the Father," 58.

5. Sara Maitland, *A Map of the New Country* (London: Routledge and Kegan Paul, 1983), 23–24.

6. See, e.g., Ps 10:4; Prov 8:13; 29:23; Jer 49:16; Jas 4:6.

7. See Job 40:11; Jer 50:32; Dan 4:37.

8. Rosemary Haughton, *The Passionate God* (New York: Paulist Press, 1981).

9. Norman Pittenger, *The Lure of Divine Love* (New York: Pilgrim, 1979), 21.

10. Ibid., 62.

11. Elisabeth Moltmann-Wendel and Jürgen Moltmann, *Humanity in God* (London: SCM Press, 1983), 15–16.

12. Carol P. Christ, *Diving Deep and Surfacing* (Boston: Beacon, 1980), 19.

13. Valerie Saiving Goldstein, "The Human Situation: A Feminine View," *Journal of Religion* 40 (April 1960): 108.

14. Simone de Beauvoir, *The Second Sex* (trans. H. M. Parshley; London: Penguin, 1983), xxviii.

15. See the general confession in the order for Morning Prayer, in the Book of Common Prayer.

16. Sallie McFague, *Metaphorical Theology* (London: SCM Press, 1983), 185.

17. Quoted in Chung Hyun Kyung, *Struggle to Be the Sun Again* (Maryknoll, N.Y.: Orbis Books, 1990), 50.

18. See, e.g., Starhawk, *The Spiral Dance: The Rebirth of the Ancient Religion of the Goddess* (New York: Harper and Row, 1979), 79–80.

19. Ibid., 80.

20. Matt 4:19; 5:13–14; Luke 11:9; 12:57; Matt 9:22; 10:31; 15:28; Luke 7:50; 8:21; 10:41–42; John 14:17; 15:15; 15:16.

21. Joanne Carlson Brown and Rebecca Parker, *Christianity, Patriarchy, and Abuse* (Cleveland: Pilgrim, 1989), 26.

22. Ibid., 26.

23. Ibid., 3.

24. Ibid., 4.

25. Chung, *Struggle to Be the Sun Again*, 113.

26. Quoted in Chung, *Struggle to Be the Sun Again*, 107.

27. See, e.g., Rosemary Radford Ruether, *Women-Church: Theology and Practice of Feminist Liturgical Communities* (San Francisco: Harper and Row, 1986).

28. Riane Eisler, *The Chalice and the Blade* (New York: Harper and Row, 1987), 203.

CHAPTER 5
Wilderness: Letting Go

AFTER TWO YEARS IN MONTREAL I moved with David and our infant son Tom to northern Ontario to take up a position jointly with David as rector of an Anglican church. Culturally, it was a move from a cosmopolitan city to a conservative paper mill town. Ecclesiastically it meant the responsibility of leadership after five years as assistant clergy in England and Québec. Spiritually the move north was the start of an inner journey into a harsher, lonelier climate, which became for me a wilderness place.

Our new parish was a community in transition, and grief, as we eventually came to realize, was woven through the fabric of people's lives. What had once been a prosperous mill town, built out of nothing and proudly known as "the model city of the north," was now a fragile and divided community. The economic viability of the mill—the town's major employer—was in question, and among the English-speaking population there was a loss of vitality and status as young people left the town to be educated and find work further south, and as the French-speaking population became the majority and shifted the former balance of power. Many who attended the Anglican church looked to it as a symbol of the good old days, when Canada was British, the town was flourishing, and English was heard in the stores and on the streets. Tradition meant identity and security; change was to be resisted.

David and I, on the other hand, had arrived with bright ideas about leading the church into an exciting future. We were modeling a new style of ministry based on partnership, as we shared the roles of parent and priest equally; we were eager to reach out to the indigenous and Francophone populations; and we believed passionately in lay ministry, inclusive liturgical language, and the full participation of children at the Eucharist. When our vision was met with misunderstanding or opposition, the conflict that resulted was deeply painful for all of us. It was humbling, sometimes humiliating, to realize that we did not have the answers for this community, and to see the congregation slowly shrink in numbers despite our best efforts. There was self-doubt as we questioned whether we had the gifts and skills needed to be in ministry in this place. The sense of disillusionment was hard to bear.

At the same time, I was continuing to read feminist theology and open up my spiritual life to its implications. God as Mother had become central to my prayers, especially since the birth of our son. The biblical references I had gathered together and written about in seminary, imaging God as midwife, woman in labor, and nursing mother, now had a new depth of meaning for me based on my own experience. The intense, visceral love I felt for my baby, which enabled me to tolerate a level of fatigue I had never known before, was an emotion that both awed and exhilarated me. To call it a divine love did not seem inappropriate. There were times, especially very late at night, when I would sit rocking and breast-feeding my son in a silent house with darkness wrapped around us, acutely aware of the bond we shared and of the way in which I was joined with mothers throughout the world and across time who had rocked and nursed their babies like this. To see myself as held in God's arms and loved so deeply was to approach an intimacy with God that I had barely glimpsed previously.

When my second pregnancy ended in a miscarriage I was shocked and broken-hearted. Having sailed through my first pregnancy, I had blithely assumed that all would be well the second time, and the loss seemed unbearable. I had visualized a daughter growing within me, and I grieved her death with a sense of aching emptiness and failure. Months later, pregnant again but unable to shake off the lonely sadness, I was sitting in the church by myself, weeping and staring at a crucifix on the wall. Quite suddenly and without any willed imagination on my part, I could picture the outstretched arms of Jesus on the cross coming forward and folding to cradle the tiny body of my miscarried child, and the face was no longer that of a crucified man dying in pain but the face of an infinitely compassionate God receiving my child, welcoming her back, and bathing my woundedness and sense of loss with a deep comfort and peace. In that moment, which happened in a split second but is a vision etched on my soul, a profound healing occurred as I was touched by a motherly God who was not a theological concept but an experienced reality.

But these were revelations of a very personal kind. Although I could draw on my spirituality and experience when engaged in pastoral work, the words I said as a vestment-clad priest on Sunday mornings often seemed at odds. With its book-based liturgies, Anglicanism is a difficult vehicle to adapt, and revisions are made to the texts slowly and tentatively. In this conservative parish, departure from the text was discouraged and alternative liturgical material viewed with suspicion. As a result, I found myself standing at the altar saying words I no longer believed, or which conveyed images that no longer carried meaning for me. In the Eucharist, for instance, even in its revised form,[1] God is consistently named as "Father," "Lord," "Almighty," and "God of power and might," with masculine pronouns throughout.

There is no hint of the possibility of feminine or nonanthropomorphic imagery. I made small linguistic changes where I could (replacing "God of power and might" with "God of mercy and light" under my breath), and in my preaching I ventured to speak of the feminine face of God, but I felt increasingly that I was split between my church persona and my inner spiritual life. I worried that I was losing my integrity—not in the moral sense, but in the sense of losing inner and outer unity or consistency—and I was aware that at the very least I was developing an ecclesiastical form of a multiple personality disorder.

Mary Daly's words to me about the impossibility of women changing the church from the inside haunted me, and I began to wonder whether I should abandon ordained ministry after all. Alternatively, I pictured myself as having gone out on such a limb theologically and spiritually that the branch had broken off and I no longer belonged. Yet there were also indications that I should stay, that I was not crazy or wrong: A woman colleague (geographically the closest, at a mere two-hour drive away!) began to meet regularly with me to share her thoughts and questions, once we discovered that we held much in common; a male colleague, whom I had wrongly supposed to be theologically conservative and therefore potentially critical, confided that although he could not always understand me, he knew there was something life-giving in what I was trying to say and do. I met others who had left the church and given up on formal religion but who had new hope that faith might be possible if it were reimaged and set free from obsolete theology. David, too, gave me courage and companionship as he struggled to be open to the (often uncomfortable) insights of feminism, as he learned to be a very present father, and as he discovered his own inner feminine. We plowed on together, side by side if not in each other's shoes, and determined that we would not leave that ministry until we had learned what it had to teach us.

During that period, in a time of meditation as I was pondering where I belonged and where I was going in my spiritual journey, an image came to me of a woman walking away from a city on a hill into a wilderness. The city was built around a cathedral which stood at its heart, on the highest point of the hill. It was not unlike Durham, where I had attended university, or, more strikingly, like Mont-Saint-Michel in France, which I had visited twice. It was away from this "city of light"[2] with its streets, people, religion, and bustling life that the woman was steadily walking, and into a lower region of sandy bush and scrub. I recognized the woman as myself and her movement into the wilderness as a symbol for my journey. Seeing her walking in that direction made me realize that I had no choice to make; the journey was already underway. I had already left the "faith of our fathers" with its massive constructions and confident dominance, symbolized by the elevated cathedral. Now I was heading into a very different place, unmarked by roads or signposts, charted by no maps, wild and rugged. There was no clear destination in view, and at first I could see no other people there, or signs of life.

But as I sat with the image, pondered it, and even tried to paint it, I saw that there were one or two other pilgrims on their journey through it, and there were small plants, flowers, and animals. What had at first seemed inhospitable, frightening terrain was in fact strangely beautiful, even friendly. But to leave the cathedral city behind—a place I had loved, where I was known and had grown up—that was a wrenching departure.

Like the image of the crucified Jesus cradling my baby in his arms, the image of the city and the wilderness flashed into my consciousness in a moment of prayer, but it has remained as an icon for meditation over many years now. I believe it conveys a truth that lies at the heart of the spiritual quest—the truth of letting go. Our calling is often to leave behind the familiar and the safe, and to go where certainty is absent and order gives way to chaos. We may believe we are heading for the promised land, but the reality is more like being lost. It is a theme deeply embedded in the biblical tradition, where it is associated with trials, hardships, and divine guidance.

Entering the Wilderness

Abraham and Sarah were called to leave the known and journey into the unknown. The opening verse of the chapter describing God's call to them seems almost to be rubbing in the necessity to leave behind all that is familiar:

> Now the LORD said to Abram, "Go from your country and your kindred and your father's house to the land that I will show you. . . . So Abram went, as the LORD had told him. . . . Abram took his wife Sarai . . . and they set forth to go to the land of Canaan. (Gen 12:1, 4–5)

Similarly, the people of Israel endured forty turbulent years in the wilderness after their exodus from slavery in Egypt, before entering the promised land:

> Remember the long way that the LORD your God has led you these forty years in the wilderness, in order to humble you, testing you to know what was in your heart. (Deut 8:2; cf. 8:15)

The wilderness was terrifying; it was a dangerous, uncharted place. But God protected the faithful:

> [God] sustained [Jacob] in a desert land,
>   in a howling wilderness waste;
> he shielded him, cared for him,

> guarded him as the apple of his eye.
> As an eagle stirs up her nest,
> and hovers over her young;
> as she spreads her wings, takes them up,
> and bears them aloft on her pinions,
> the LORD alone guided him. (Deut 32:10–12, altered slightly)

Significantly, the Gospels attest that Jesus underwent a forty-day period of isolation, temptation, prayer, and fasting in the wilderness after his baptism and prior to beginning his public ministry:

> The Spirit immediately drove [Jesus] out into the wilderness. He was in the wilderness forty days, tempted by Satan; and he was with the wild beasts; and angels waited on him. (Mark 1:12–13)

The paradox is that although God is said to call us, lead us, or drive us out into the wilderness, our inclination is to turn and flee. The Israelites found the wilderness so unnerving, with its apparent barrenness and their terror of dying there, that they raged at Moses and told him they would rather have died as slaves in Egypt (Exod 16:2–3). The wilderness is the realm named by Jung as "the shadow." It is the realm of the unconscious, of suppressed fears and longings; it lies out of sight, unknown by the conscious mind, erupting only in dreams, compulsions, psychoses. Until it is entered and explored (brought to consciousness), it remains associated with death, terror, evil, darkness. It seems wild and untamed, hostile to normal life. It harbors "wild beasts," strange freaks of nature and criminals or outcasts. Because it appears to be so dangerous, our instincts scream at us to stay away, to keep close to the light of the city, to bar the doors and windows to the wildness and the dark.

Poet Mary Oliver writes of the terrifying power of natural forces—thunder, cyclone, fire, tornado, flood—that often are symbolic of the wilderness:

> Everyone knows the great energies running amok cast
> terrifying shadows.[3]

Wisdom asks us to stay in the wilderness because it is the sacred place of transformation. Mystics know it as the dark night of the soul. Theologians have named it the *via negativa*—the way of negation, of letting go, of mystery. Jungians speak of embracing the shadow there, in order for full psychological integration to be possible. Buddhists teach the wisdom of no escape or nonattachment, of *sunyata* or emptiness.[4] Feminist spirituality recognizes that the terrifying figure of the witch on the heath is none other than the ancient wisdom of the feminine. These teachings, profound but not popular, ancient but uncommon, have been companions for me through wilderness times. Each has been life giving, often providing guidance when I have felt most alone. They are stars in a dark night sky.

The Dark Night of the Soul in Mysticism

Mystics know that to go deeper into God we have to let go and enter a place of darkness and silence. It is very different from our post-Enlightenment, post–Industrial Revolution, post–technological revolution world of neon lights, twenty-four-hour shifts, constant noise, and all-night stores and entertainment. We have made darkness optional; total darkness in the city is impossible to find. Shooting stars may flash overhead, but in the orange glow of urban night we are blind to them. Silence is almost taboo; as we work, wait, shop, travel, cook, or eat, we surround ourselves with sound. It is no surprise that places of silence and stillness are being sought out as people retreat from the noise to try to find spiritual refreshment.

For the mystic, the darkness of pain and doubt is not to be avoided or denied but entered into. John of the Cross (1542–1591) wrote that all creativity, all nurture, all enlightenment, all true strength comes "by night."[5] Nicholas of Cusa (1401–1464) criticized the overrational tendency of scholars or academics, "in that they are afraid to enter the darkness. Reason shuns it and is afraid to steal in. But in avoiding the darkness, reason does not arrive at a vision of the invisible."[6] In the wilderness we are searching for the invisible, the unknown, the ineffable. Our destination cannot be seen, and our usual skills and faculties are redundant. It is a time of waiting, described hauntingly by poet T. S. Eliot as "the darkness of God" when even faith, hope, and love must wait.[7]

Darkness has always been part of my spiritual life. As a teenager I had grown up with God from my mother's arms, but I still sensed a yearning for God that was unsatisfied. While my Christian friends were enjoying the born-again, brightly lit certainty of faith following conversion, I was reading my mother's copy of the Christian mystical classic *The Cloud of Unknowing*, and sensing I was to follow a different path. Years later I came upon Eliot's lines on waiting in the darkness of God and welcomed them as an anchor in prayer when all other words failed me. At that time David and I had converted a tiny basement storage room—no more than a closet—into a prayer space in our home. It was dark, down under the vivacious activity of the rest of the house, and close to the earth. In that chapel of silence I would read the poetry over and over until I knew it by heart, and would pray the prayer of waiting in the darkness.

It is in the experience of the mystics, not the dwellers in the city of light, that "God is met in dazzling darkness." God's covenant with Abraham and Sarah was made in "a deep and terrifying darkness" (Gen 15:12); Jacob saw God face to face in the presence of an angel who wrestled with him in the darkness for one long night (Gen 32:24–31); God spoke out of "thick darkness" to Moses when the Ten

Commandments were given (Deut 5:22); and the psalmist acknowledges that in a mysterious way "the night is as bright as the day" (Ps 139:12) to God. Indeed, we celebrate the coming of God to dwell among us at the darkest time of the year. The Sun of Righteousness, the Light of the World, comes forth from the darkness of the womb into the darkness of night during the depths of winter. Darkness can be trusted, for God is there. "It is in darkness that birth takes place," writes Joanna Macy.[8]

The *Via Negativa*

Matthew Fox, theologian, priest, and founder of the Institute in Culture and Creation Spirituality, has developed a full spirituality and theology of the *via negativa*, or the path of mystery, darkness, silence, and suffering. He does not glorify suffering or see it as God's punishment or test for us, but recognizes that it is part of our lives and as such can be integrated and transformed rather than dreaded or anaesthetized. In his groundbreaking book *Original Blessing* he presents the four interconnected paths of the spiraling spiritual journey: the *via positiva* of befriending creation, loving it, trusting it, and recognizing ourselves not as separate from it but part of it; the *via negativa* of befriending darkness and letting go, letting be, and sinking into the silent depths of God; the *via creativa* of befriending creativity through spiritual practices such as art, meditation, dance, and music, where we cocreate with God; and the *via transformativa* of befriending the new creation through acts of justice, compassion, and celebration, so that all we do and are joins with the creativity of the Holy Spirit.

Of the *via negativa* Fox writes: "We all began in the dark. . . . The womb was dark and not fearful. These are our origins, the very holy origin of our original being, our original blessedness. There is no underestimating the importance of our meditating on our dark and silent origins if we are to make touch with our spiritual depths."[9] This path is a path of emptying and of being emptied; of befriending the darkness and learning how to enter into our pain in order to "burn it as fuel for our journey."[10] It is not a masochistic path, but a realistic and hopeful one that faces the darkness and suffering of life, embraces it, and journeys through it to a deeper knowing and a deeper loving. Fox quotes Mechtild of Magdeburg (ca. 1210–1280):

> When you drink the waters of sorrow
> you shall kindle the fire of love
> with the match of perseverance—
> This is the way to dwell in the desert.[11]

Unlike a theology that focuses on "the fall," original sin, and our wretchedness and unworthiness, which teaches mortification of the flesh to control it and sees suffering as the wages for sin, the *via negativa* of this spirituality of "original blessing" sees suffering as the birth pangs of a universe and celebrates all of creation, darkness included, as good and blessed.

Medieval theologian Meister Eckhart wrote:

> What is this darkness? What is its name?
> Call it: an aptitude for sensitivity.
> Call it: a rich sensitivity which will make you whole.
> Call it: your potential for vulnerability.[12]

The *via negativa* teaches us receptivity, both to our own pain and to that of others. It births compassion. It is not sent to try us, but comes by virtue of our being alive. Sin is a refusal to feel, to be alive, to be vulnerable. Sin is clinging, controlling, projecting, avoiding. As Fox writes, "The refusal to trust, to trust the buoyancy of the water, of the darkness, of the pain, of the nothingness, of the God of nothingness, of our own body, own air, own lungs, own trust—all this is sinful because it stifles our spiritual growth."[13] On this path salvation is not escape *from* pain, but journey *through* pain. And "forgiveness is another word for letting go" as we stop clinging to guilt, fear, and control.[14]

By following the path of letting go and befriending darkness, we cease to be victims and learn what it is to bring creativity and transformation to birth. Darkness, writes Fox, "is the origin of everything that is born—stars born in the darkness of space, our ideas and images born in the darkness of the brain, children born from the darkness of their mothers' wombs, movements of liberation born from the darkness of slavery and pain."[15]

I read Fox's *Original Blessing* while in ministry in the north. It was my practice to say evening prayers in the church at the end of each day, and to read for a while in the solitary silence. I treasured those times as oases of peace and refreshment, especially during the turbulence of handling parish conflict and in the unremitting busyness of parenthood interwoven with ministry. Fox's book gave me the courage not to flee. As I felt myself pulled in two directions (public church persona versus private spiritual unfolding) I learned a little more about trusting the process and giving up the need to control it. Mirroring this movement toward letting go, I dreamed one night that I was getting off a runaway snowmobile which was hurtling noisily through snow-covered bush, and instead I began to make my journey on foot. I woke with a sense of calm and the knowledge that even the *via negativa* is essentially benign.

Bringing the Shadow to Consciousness: Jungian Wisdom

Jung maintained that almost all psychological disorders have a spiritual malaise at root, based on an inner conflict between the ego or conscious aspect, and the shadow or unconscious. He believed that for spiritual, psychological, and physical well-being it is necessary for the two to be integrated, but he recognized that we are tremendously resistant to the process of integration. Like the terror of entering the darkness or journeying through the wilderness, we fear the shadow within ourselves and do all we can to keep it locked away or project it onto others as our enemy. The fundamental question, according to Jung, is how to "love the enemy in [one's] own heart and call the wolf [one's] brother."[16] He observed that although Christians are taught to love their enemy and serve the poor, when we encounter the enemy within, a different dynamic arises: "We . . . condemn and rage against ourselves. We hide it from the world; we refuse to admit ever having met this least among the lowly in ourselves. Had it been God himself who drew near to us in this despicable form, we should have denied him a thousand times before a single cock had crowed."[17] Rejecting the shadow because we are "afraid to grope in the dark," we suffer from lack of faith, love, hope, and understanding.

Jungian analyst Marion Woodman uses the analogies of the chrysalis, the pregnant virgin, and the Black Madonna to describe the process of transformation that can occur in the wilderness. Within the chrysalis, encased in its outer shell, immobile, apparently dead, something new and beautiful is being made, if only we will trust it. "The chrysalis is essential if we are to find ourselves," writes Woodman. "That is what going into the chrysalis is all about—undergoing a metamorphosis in order one day to be able to stand up and say *I am*."[18] It is a movement inward, into silence, stillness, and shadow, in order to become free to be more fully and magnificently alive. Like the *via negativa* and the dark night of the soul, it is an acceptance of change, mystery, birth, and death.

The pregnant virgin and Black Madonna are also powerful symbols of this process. As Woodman explains: "Both men and women are searching for their pregnant virgin. She is the part of us who is outcast, the part who comes to consciousness through going into darkness, mining our leaden darkness, until we bring her silver out."[19] The image of the Black Madonna, such as the twelfth-century Byzantine sculpture in Montserrat, Spain, represents for Woodman the strong, integrated wisdom in feminine form that embraces both spirit and body, life and death, light and darkness. She is the Goddess we encounter if we have the wisdom and courage to walk away from the city of light into the unknown land of the shadow. She is described in an ancient fragment of text entitled *The Thunder, Perfect Mind*, from a second-century CE Gnostic community:

> For I am the first and the last.
> I am the honored one and the scorned one.
> I am the whore and the holy one.
> I am the wife and the virgin.
> I am [the mother] and the daughter

I am the silence that is incomprehensible

. . . .

I am the utterance of my name.[20]

For Christians the season of Advent can become symbolic of this journey to soul-birth. Mariann Burke, a Jungian therapist and member of the Religious of the Sacred Heart, writes that "during Advent the way leads to the wilderness."[21] As we wrestle with our demons there, a new life can be born. Mark's Gospel begins with this proclamation from Isaiah:

> The voice of one crying out in the wilderness:
>   "Prepare the way of the Lord,
>   make his paths straight." (Mark 1:3)

In our wilderness we prepare for the birth of the divine child within, the inner self that is created in the divine image and called away from convention or constriction to fullness of life and overflowing compassion. The wilderness is a place apart, but it is a holy place. As Burke comments: "Jung was fond of saying that we do not transform the shadow by imagining figures of light but through experiencing the darkness. In Christian tradition, the experience of the inner divine child as the recovery of an aspect of ourselves is the fruit of the sojourn in the wilderness."[22]

Awakening and Letting Go: The Buddhist Path

"When you . . . become a Buddhist, you become a refugee," writes Buddhist nun Pema Chödrön.[23] The image of the homeless wanderer is central to Buddhism, with its teachings about letting go, nonattachment, nonself, and non-permanence. That which we can hold on to becomes our cocoon, trapping us in safety and a half life that is constantly fleeing pain and seeking pleasure but avoiding the Now, avoiding what Buddhist author Thich Nhat Hanh calls the miracle of the present moment. Enlightenment is not a blissful state of constant joy, but is, rather, attentiveness, being awake, being open to all that is, whether joyful or painful. When the Buddha was asked once, "Are you human or are you a god?" he is said to have replied, "I am awake."

During times of difficulty, darkness, or suffering, Buddhism does not teach resistance to these in the sense of seeking escape, but a gentle opening to them so that understanding and compassion can enter and fear can dissolve. Chödrön uses the analogy of ravens riding on the wind:

> How do we work with this tendency to block and to freeze and to refuse to take
> another step toward the unknown? . . . How do we learn to open that door and
> step through it again and again, so that life becomes a process of growing up,

becoming more and more fearless and flexible, more and more able to play like a raven in the wind? The wilder the weather is, the more the ravens love it. . . . They challenge the wind . . . they play on it, they float on it. In order to exist here [i.e., Cape Breton], they have had to develop a zest for challenge and for life. . . . It adds up to tremendous beauty and inspiration and uplifted feeling. The same goes for us.[24]

Wilderness, like wild, icy winds, frightens us. We tend to want to flee, or cocoon—anything rather than accept it for what it is and enter into it. Chödrön calls it an experience of being thrown out of the nest, or being in the *bardo* state, a state of transition usually between death and the next rebirth in Buddhist philosophy but also referring to the time between glimpsing the right path (hearing of the promised land, leaving the city of light) and reaching it: "You've left the shore, but you haven't arrived anywhere yet. You don't know where you're going. . . . You've become home-less, you long to go back, but there's no way to go back."[25]

Being here in *bardo*, in the wilderness, trying to ride on the wind, letting go of old securities and fears, awake to what is, is the warrior's journey in Buddhism. This is the strong, compassionate, wholehearted warrior, akin to Joseph Campbell's archetypal hero. She or he does not attack what seems negative, but seeks to *know* it more fully, in order to embrace and transform it. "We need not chase away evil," writes Thich Nhat Hanh. "We can embrace and transform it in a non-violent, non-dualistic way."[26]

Nhat Hanh equates the Buddhist concept of *nirvana* with the Christian image of the kingdom of heaven: Both stand for absolute reality, the ultimate, the ground of our being. They are not future places to which we escape or earn our way, but are states of being now to which we awaken. And the path involves letting go of our fears, cravings, attachments, illusions and ideas—even our ideas about God or Buddha. As we learn emptiness, it becomes possible to ride on the wind and be blown into the wilderness without terror.

Voices of the Crone

Feminists are rediscovering and celebrating the shadowy wisdom of the wise old woman, once known and revered as the hag ("wise one") or crone. What became distorted and demonized as the witchy face of evil was once recognized as ancient feminine sacred knowledge. Before light became associated with God and darkness with evil, before fears of chaos, darkness, and sinfulness were projected onto women, once upon a time woman's wisdom was consulted from the dark mysterious depths. Our Neolithic ancestors painted red ochre around the vulva-shaped openings into the underground passages and caves where they painted their sacred art; they were entering the Great Mother, in all her dark mystery. In mythology the crone was to be found apart, away from daily life, in a hut in the middle of a forest, or on a heath at night, or in a cave. She was not beautiful but lined with age, experience, and wisdom; she was not youthful and virginal but strong with a maternal wiriness and endurance; she could be terrifying, she could make seemingly impossible demands, but she had the secret to the puzzle, the key to the tower, the answer to the riddle.[27]

The crone knows about death and does not fear it. She knows about loss and decay, and understands that they are part of the cycle of life. She often sits at the crossroads and points to the steep, difficult path. She comes to the deathbed and the birthing place. A culture such as ours, with its fear of death, avoidance of darkness, and requirement that women be young and beautiful, cannot know her or her wisdom. But Starhawk describes how the crone is revered in Wicca as a symbol of the sacred feminine to this day:

> She is the Old Woman, the Crone who has passed menopause, the power of ending, of death. . . . Life feeds on death—death leads on to life, and in that knowledge lies wisdom. The Crone is the Wise Woman, infinitely old. . . . Most of us live removed from nature, cut off from the experiences that constantly remind more "primitive" people that every act of creation is an act of aggression. To plant a garden, you must dig out the weeds. . . . To write a book, you must destroy draft after draft of your own work. . . . Creation postulates change; and any change destroys what went before.[28]

We need the crone. Feminist spirituality does not propose replacing God the Father with a nubile young goddess in a sexually trivializing way. Nor does it paint a sentimental picture of the world as sugar and spice and all things nice. The crone represents the earthy, wrinkled presence of the Divine in the drama and the dirt of our lives—a Washerwoman God cleaning up our mess,[29] a Grandmother God passing on her wisdom, a God who looks like the mothers and grandmothers of the "disappeared" in South America indomitably parading the streets for justice. She is like the widow in Jesus' parable who refused to take No for an answer in her demand for justice (Luke 18:1–8).

Today, in the informal circles of women meeting together for spiritual community and mutual support, many older women are creating croning ceremonies for themselves and each other as they reach the age of menopause or become seniors. The ceremonies affirm the goodness and strength of older women, and celebrate their wisdom and creativity. They counteract the message of our culture that an older woman is undesirable, ugly, or useless.

Two images in particular speak to me of the Holy Crone. One, cut out from a newspaper and pasted onto the folder containing the first drafts of this book, is a photograph of a seventy-eight-year-old Kosovar woman, Shefkete Ukshini, comforting her crying, frightened grandson Ilir, eight years old. They are both refugees from

Kosovo, driven out of their homes with thousands of others by Serbian forces. She has a shawl over her head, and the face that looks out from underneath it at her grandson is wrinkled and bony. Her face is pressed close to his, and she is kissing his cheek. Her hand, rough and strong, is against his other cheek as he shuts his eyes and cries. She cannot make the fighting stop; she is just another powerless old woman, on one level. But the compassion on her face and the tenderness in her gesture move me to tears and give me an idea of how God as Holy Crone is present to us.

The other image comes in words. I saw them on a T-shirt, concise and without need of explanation: "Older, Wiser and Slightly More Dangerous." I had turned forty not long before, and had begun to write. But I was afraid of the potential responses to my writing from those who would see it as unchristian, even heretical. The slogan delighted me; it offered me an invitation to embrace who I was becoming without apologies or defensiveness. It described the essential nature of the Holy Crone with her wisdom culled from experience, her freedom from convention, and her love of rocking the boat. She is dangerous, and so is her journey, but she is not malign. She rattles and goads, encourages and emboldens. She dares to say Yes, when all around the voices are saying, "You'd better not."

At home in the wilderness, along with the mystic, the *via negativa* theologian, the Jungian, the Buddhist, and the refugee from the city of light, is the crone. It is not, after all, a completely solitary place.

The Inner Journey

What makes the wilderness way such a difficult one is that it is an inner journey which ultimately we have to undergo for ourselves. Like birth and death, no one can do this for us. There are, as we have seen, companions to go with us, but whereas in the city of light we receive encouragement and praise for struggling to climb the ladder, be productive, attain success, or be a winner, when we walk away we may find that we do so unnoticed and unblessed. We may also encounter resistance to the journey not only from within but from outside, too, as those who think they know us criticize our changes or beg us to stay the same.

The quest is fraught with paradoxes. On the one hand, it is a reaching beyond the self to the mystery of the Other; on the other hand, it is a reclaiming and deeper knowing of the self who is a divine creation. It involves finding one's voice and speaking one's truth, as well as being silent or struck dumb. It is a willingness to let go and experience nothingness, while at the same time being a discovery of new gifts with fresh insights. But paradox is the earth from which wisdom manifests itself. As two apparently contradictory forces pull and stretch apart, a third arises that transcends and unifies the opposites. As Marion Woodman says, "Spiritual birth, like biological birth, requires a union of opposites, from which the sacred child is born."[30]

Awakening

Carol Christ describes the beginning of the journey for women as an awakening, and she recognizes the obstacles women face in this, as well as the paradoxical nature of the journey, when it seems sometimes as if all of history, nature, and even the gods are against it. The start, she says, is not conversion so much as waking up:

> "Awakening" suggests that the self needs only to notice what is already there. Awakening implies that the ability to see or to know is within the self, once the sleeping draft is refused. . . . For women, awakening is not so much a giving up as a gaining of power . . . a coming to self . . . a grounding of selfhood in the powers of being, rather than a surrender of self.[31]

Awakening rarely happens once, in a decisive moment. There are usually repeated times of waking up—a sudden jolting realization, a chance conversation, an experience which cracks the chrysalis, a thought which makes the pit of the stomach lurch. Going back to sleep may be a possibility and an attractive escape, but there is often a feeling deep inside, even as life is apparently going on as usual on the surface, that there is no going back. Awakening is therefore a leaving and a letting go, unless fear brings denial creeping in and sleep returns. Awakening can also feel more like a death than a birth, as we become aware of what we are leaving behind. It sometimes requires a grieving period before active journeying is possible.

My mother died while I was in my northern Ontario wilderness. She was still several years from retirement, a busy and well-loved family physician, and a grandmother to an increasing number of young children as my sisters and I had our babies. Diagnosed with advanced cancer in the early autumn, she died before Christmas. In the midst of my anger and pain—deeply sorry, too, for my father who was now suddenly alone—I turned to God for comfort. I believed that my mother was with God, more fully than had been possible during her life; I expected to find consolation in that faith. But instead I found only a void. It was as though in place of my faith there was a gaping hole that had engulfed both my God and my mother. I remember walking one night in an empty park, wailing out loud to the darkness as I felt this loss—the abandonment of a motherless child and a soul adrift in a meaningless universe.

Yet this experience was an awakening. I had been striving to develop a deeper, closer relationship with my mother, and I had been praying for a more profound knowledge of God. Both became possible only after my mother's death. "I pray God to rid me of 'God,'" wrote Meister Eckhart, longing to be free of concepts and limiting constructs in order to encounter the Divine beyond theology.[32] "God is nothing. God is no thing, God is nothingness; and yet God is something."[33] This was my experience as I cried in the night. "Think of the soul as a vortex or a whirlwind," Eckhart explains, "and you will understand how we are to sink eternally from negation to negation into the one; and how we are to sink eternally from letting go to letting go into God."[34] Thus, mysteriously, in the midst of the wilderness of awakening and dying, "God's exit is her entrance."[35]

It is now more than a decade since both my parents died, and I know myself to be an orphan, to be no one's daughter, to be marked for life by bereavement. But the scar is not an open wound, and I see myself linked inextricably with my parents, woven through with their lives, their stories, their likeness, their fragile and ordinary flesh and blood. The letting go and the mourning were necessary before the deeper connection with them as part of me became possible.

So it is with God. It has only been as I have lost God, over and over again, that I have found faith. Images for God continue to collapse, words to fail, names to change. The awakening wind in the wilderness blows, like the Holy Spirit, where she wills, flattening our flimsy structures and pushing us always further, deeper.

In her book *The Sacred and the Feminine*, Kathryn Allen Rabuzzi describes the journey one woman makes in leaving theology to find the sacred:

> For her there is no going back to the old structures. The words *God, Heaven, Christ* no longer resonate for her. But yet . . . over a period of years, it occurs to her that she does have faith. But it is not a faith in anything she has words to name. She does not believe in heaven or hell. She does not go to church. Yet something in her life serves as a conduit to a level of experience she recognizes as sacred.[36]

Awakening and letting go in the wilderness is a constant process of bumping up against "and yet." We mourn, and yet we discover new life; we leave, and yet we come home to ourselves; we are struck dumb, and yet (like Zechariah, father of John the Baptist) we encounter a birth and are called to name it (see Luke 1:5–25, 57–80). All the time the discovery is not conceptual but experiential; the journey is uniquely ours. Naomi Goldenberg writes that great founders of religions such as Jesus, the Buddha, and Muhammad underwent profound spiritual and personal experiences, with extraordinary degrees of commitment and single-mindedness, as they followed their vision. Their disciples, by contrast, could only make a "pale imitation" of the leader unless they too discovered their own vision.[37]

We look for a leader to follow when we are lost. We want to believe that someone somewhere has a map, and if we could only follow the directions we would soon get out of the wilderness and check in at the promised land. The truth is, there are no shortcuts through; but neither are there any dead ends. The medieval pilgrims who could not undertake the journey to the Holy Land sometimes made a symbolic pilgrimage by walking a huge labyrinth, laid out in a floor design in cathedrals such as in Chartres, France. The labyrinth had no intersections where a right way had to be chosen, and no dead ends where the path ended. The pilgrim simply had to follow the elaborate windings of one path to and fro, around and around, sometimes coming close to the center, sometimes curving away, until it led right through the pattern and out again.

With its ancient pre-Christian roots in the initiation mysteries of the old religions, the labyrinth symbolizes the spiritual journey we are invited to make. Not surprisingly, the sacred path of the labyrinth as a form of prayer or meditation is being rediscovered now, often in conjunction with women's retreats, holistic health centers, Goddess spirituality, meditative worship services, and other alternatives to the rationalist, linear ways of patriarchy. Labyrinths are being built once more on hilltops, in gardens, in churches and hospitals. As today's pilgrims walk them, they are searching not for the Holy Land but for healing and peace, not for Jerusalem but for meaning.

In her book *Walking a Sacred Path: Rediscovering the Labyrinth as a Spiritual Tool*, Lauren Artress, an Episcopal priest, describes the labyrinth as a sacred space in which we can focus our attention "and listen to the longing of the soul."[38] She sees its contemporary rediscovery as a gift that can provide "a watering hole for the human spirit, a deep channel for the human soul."[39] She leads labyrinth walks, retreats, and educational events for the pilgrims of today who, in North America at least, are largely without direction and support on the spiritual path. And she welcomes the labyrinth as a valuable guide: "The labyrinth is an old watercourse that dried up over time and circumstance. But it is filling again now, with clear, cool waters. It is inviting us to drink. The labyrinth has been awaiting rediscovery, longing to guide us, awaken us while we walk this earthly path. The time has come."[40]

Befriending Death

In a dualistic culture, death is the ultimate enemy. It is seen as the opposite of life, an affront, a thief. Death defies human attempts at control, and signals failure, unless it is seized and inflicted violently upon others. Chung Hyun Kyung describes the society of developed countries as death-centered because at the same time they fear and flee from death they are fascinated by it, producing weapons of mass destruction, threatening political enemies with death, killing the ecosystem, using violent death as entertainment, and staring unflinchingly at images of death from around the world in the media. We project onto others what we fear for ourselves, and we desensitize ourselves to the atrocities that we create.

A religion based on dualistic thinking offers an escape from death, the earth, and physicality into an otherworldly realm of eternal life and light. Thus, in the Christian Scriptures we read:

> Then I saw a new heaven and a new earth; for the first heaven and the first earth
> had passed away, and the sea was no more. And I saw the holy city, the new

Jerusalem, coming down out of heaven from God. . . . And I heard a loud voice from the throne, saying, . . . "Death will be no more" . . . And the city has no need of sun or moon to shine on it, for the glory of God is its light. . . . There will be no night there. . . . [God's] servants will worship him . . . and they will reign forever and ever. (Rev 21:1–4, 23, 25; 22:3, 5)

The last enemy to be destroyed is death. (1 Cor 15:26)

We will not all die, but we will all be changed. . . . Then the saying that is written will be fulfilled:

> "Death has been swallowed up in victory."
> "Where, O death, is your victory?"
> Where, O death, is your sting?" (1 Cor 15:51, 54–55)

Our Savior Christ Jesus . . . abolished death and brought life and immortality to light through the gospel. (2 Tim 1:10)

Because death is seen as the result of sin, it has no place in the realm of salvation.[41] Mortality and physicality alike are shunned as ungodly. As Simone de Beauvoir evocatively wrote:

Man is in revolt against his carnal state; he sees himself as a fallen god: his curse is to be fallen from a bright and ordered heaven into the chaotic shadows of his mother's womb [i.e., earth, mortality]. . . . This quivering jelly which is elaborated in the womb (the womb, secret and sealed like the tomb) evokes too clearly the soft viscosity of carrion for him not to turn shuddering away.[42]

Ruether describes this antideath dualism as a "theology of rebellion into infinity," where the "self-infinitizing spirit" seeks to be autonomous, immortal, and omnipotent, escaping the natural world with its cycle of life, death, and regeneration, and in fact destroying that world along with all other "enemies."[43] In Judeo-Christian history it was as the transcendent male God repressed the "pagan" deities of the cycles of life and promised a new creation without death that a deep and destructive dualism became enshrined: "So the pattern of death and resurrection was cut loose from organic harmonies and became instead an historical pattern of wrath and redemption. . . . The prophetic drive to free man from nature ended in the apocalyptic negation of history itself: a cataclysmic world destruction and angelic new creation."[44] Ruether calls for a new understanding of salvation as reconciliation with our humanity, mortality, and place in nature, rather than as escape from these. In such an understanding death would no longer be feared, resisted, or used as a weapon, but accepted as a friend that completes the natural cycle of the human soul.

In the wilderness we encounter death—our own mortality and fragility; the little deaths of letting go of old securities; the natural pattern of growth, productivity, death, and decay that is enacted daily around us—if we pay attention and notice it. A unitive spirituality recognizes that this is so, that life and death are "a twisted vine sharing a single root."[45] It does not need a theology of the righteous being "raptured" and bodily removed out of this world to escape death and destruction, for it does not equate death with God's wrath. Instead, like Francis of Assisi, it can praise God for "sister Death-of-Body from whom no man living will escape,"[46] with acceptance and gratitude rather than dread.

According to Jungian psychologist Erich Neumann, the great archetypes for this path are feminine—the Great Round, the transformative Goddess who contains both life and death, heaven and earth, as source of all that is: "The Great Goddess is the flowing unity of subterranean and celestial primordial water . . . the circular life-generating ocean above and below the earth. . . . She is the ocean of life with its life-and-death-bringing seasons."[47] She is symbolized as the goddess Isis, embracing Osiris and all the dead, and as Mary the mother of Jesus holding her dead son in her lap. Death is part of the whole, and a unitive feminine wisdom knows this.

It is not surprising that the modern hospice movement, a movement that has befriended death in the medical world, has women as its pioneers. Recovering the ancient wisdom of the healing women who attended births, sickness, and death before a male medical profession seized control and relegated women to the serving role as nurses, female physicians such as Cicely Saunders and my mother, Marjorie Reid, have worked to change the attitude of their colleagues toward the dying patient, and to change the way in which terminal care is carried out, by founding hospices. The hospice was originally a staging post on a journey, a place where travelers could rest and be refreshed. The name itself is a step toward befriending death as a natural part of the human experience, another step on the journey through life, not a calamitous disaster.

Hospice care today provides a very different alternative to the high-tech hospital approach to dying. In place of the isolation of a side ward, where the patient is left alone because no more can be done, or the frantic intervention of the intensive care unit, where death is fought off by whatever means possible until the last moment, the hospice environment is calm, supportive, and family centered. Pain is managed in such a way that quality of life is maintained, and death is allowed to approach naturally. Dying is no longer taboo but is spoken of, prepared for, and treated with respect. Family and friends are encouraged to be as present and involved in the care as they wish to be, rather than kept behind sterile doors to wait for the professionals to handle everything. Terminal care in a hospice may include massage, aromatherapy, music, creative writing, prayer. After my mother's death from cancer, a colleague wrote, "She died as she hoped the hospice would help others to die, in peace and faith." And the hospice she had founded and directed before her death—the Hospice of Our Lady and St. John, Willen, Buckinghamshire, England—was described by a local historian as "a haven of peace and tranquility."[48]

If death can be befriended, then indeed it loses its sting, but without being banished or fled from. Then the rituals surrounding death can, like those around birth, be returned to the family from the hands of the professionals. Then death when it comes need not be disguised or euphemized as "sleep," with cosmetics and chemical preservatives denying its reality, and the metal caskets that defy the natural processes of decay and regeneration will no longer be needed. If death is befriended, then the bereaved are set free from their isolation, for they are known to be learning the difficult art of letting go, and they are supported and understood with no discomfort or fear, no easy clichés that leapfrog over the darkness of death and prematurely seek comfort and resurrection. "Let children walk with Nature," urges author John Muir. "Let them see the beautiful blendings and communions of death and life, their joyous inseparable unity, and they will learn that death is stingless indeed, and as beautiful as life, and that the grave has no victory, for it never fights."[49]

The Unitive Path

The wilderness journey through doubt, confusion, loss, awakening, and letting go is not a trial that God requires of us, but is, rather, in Dorothee Sölle's words, "a matter of agreement and consent, of being at one with what is alive."[50] The quest is for oneness with God, with life. Our relationship to God, says Sölle, is not meant to be one of obedience but of union, and this is the fundamental purpose of religion—to bring us to oneness with the Divine. The journey is not like boot camp, where we learn to toughen up and accept harsh commands; rather, it is a pilgrimage of love.

In describing the stages of faith development, James Fowler writes that before faith can be fully and personally embraced a period of intense critical reflection must take place. This difficult stage involves stepping back from previously held beliefs and practices in order to critique them. It is often experienced as a crisis or loss of faith, as the images and certainties of childhood or young adulthood crumble and fall away. If the process is allowed to continue, however, without a rushing back to resuscitate the old faith system, then at midlife or beyond a unifying faith may emerge:

> This stage involves the embrace and integration of opposites or polarities in one's life. . . . It means recognizing that we are both masculine and feminine, with all the meanings those characteristics have in our particular culture. It may mean reintegrating our masculine and feminine modalities. . . .

Persons at [this] stage . . . have struggled (and are struggling) for freedom
from false, oversimple images of faith. They are working toward the integration
of the high and the low, in human life—the conscious and the unconscious.
They are learning to live the paradoxical truths of the gospel, that it is in giving
that we receive; it is in dying to the false self that we, by grace, are born to the
seeds of a new being.[51]

Embrace, integration, being at one—these are the movements of the journey
through the wilderness. It begins with a fall not so much into sin as into darkness,
mystery, emptiness. There can be agonizing spiritual pain, as Jesus experienced in
Gethsemane before his arrest, until the point of deep letting go is reached. Then
"Thy will be done" is spoken not as a prayer of defeat and surrender to a superior
God-knows-best deity, but as a yearning for union with the Divine so that in us the
cosmic dance of creation in all its multifaceted wonder can continue unimpeded.
Thich Nhat Hanh uses the analogy of water and waves: "Once you are capable of
touching water, you will not mind the coming and going of the waves. You are no
longer concerned about the birth and death of the wave. You are no longer afraid.
. . . You are capable of letting these ideas go because you have already touched the
water."[52]

In my own wilderness, it has not been theology that has sustained me but
poetry, images from nature, and often silence. From my childhood faith in "the
Almighty" to my feminist experiments with God as "Mother" or "she," I have
found that all human metaphors fail and God is repeatedly lost to me. One morning I was washing my face when I knew with a rush of adrenaline that I did not
believe in "God" anymore. The whole idea of a supreme being "out there" somewhere was totally implausible. It was more than the collapse of faith years before at
my first tragic funeral; that had required a reworking of my theology of God's
power and goodness, whereas this was more sweeping, more existential. It did not
have the anguish of the time when I had cried over the absence of God after my
mother's death, only a gripping gut knowledge that "God" as an external, separate
force did not exist for me any longer. Fighting panic and drawing on the calm support of Jean, my wise spiritual director, who did not seem perturbed by this, I sat
with the absence of God in my times of prayer for weeks. I believed intellectually
that waiting was more important than reconstructing, that the shedding of one
skin of faith always gives way to something new. But I had no idea what that new
thing would be.

The breakthrough occurred when I came across a line attributed to the Muslim
mystic Kabir: "I laugh when I hear that the fish in the water is thirsty." We cannot
lose God, because God is all. God is the embrace that sustains the totality of life; he
is the one in whom we live and move and have our being; she is Divine Oneness.

The wilderness pilgrim is like one who bathes in the lake by night, swims out into the deep, ceases her thrashing strokes, and quietly floats, held up by the dark water.

Moving On

After four and a half years David and I left parish ministry in the north to take up a joint appointment as ecumenical campus ministers at a university in southern Ontario. It was not the end of the wilderness; in a sense one never leaves the wilderness but becomes more familiar with its paths so that it is less fearful, even attractive. The move was a step out of conventional ministry into a context where questions, critiques, and innovations were the norm. The challenge of bringing the gospel to a secular community required departure from tradition and an openness to meeting people where they were. There was no church building in which to wait for the people to come. Although I did not know this at the beginning, it would also require a greater sense of clarity and groundedness in my own being. Without the books and rituals and vestments of tradition, which had begun to chafe so insistently, I would need to find an inner reference point and identity.

During a retreat shortly before we moved, I was praying with a gospel passage using the Ignatian method of entering with the imagination into the text. It was the story of Jesus asking Simon Peter if he loved him (John 21:15–19). I was struck by Jesus' calling Simon Peter "Simon, son of John," identifying him not by the name the church uses—that is, Peter—but by his own name and his own roots. When I imagined myself in Simon's place, being addressed by Jesus, I heard him call me by my maiden name, which I had unquestioningly given up at marriage eleven years before. To hear myself called Lucy Reid again was like being jolted by a current of electricity. This was me, not the priest, not the wife, not the mother, but my self. And it was that person, behind the various roles and masks and expectations, who was called to go into the unknown future. Leaving the north, I left my married name behind and came back to myself, my own name. It was not a feminist gesture or a rejection of David, but a homecoming. The journey of faith is always a journey home. In the wilderness we find ourselves.

Notes

1. *The Book of Alternative Services of the Anglican Church of Canada* (Toronto: Anglican Book Centre, 1985).

2. This phrase is found in the *Book of Alternative Services*, 200, to refer to the kingdom of heaven. It is based on an image in Rev 21:23.

3. Mary Oliver, "Shadows," in *Dream Work* (New York: Atlantic Monthly Press, 1986), 17.

4. See Pema Chödrön, *The Wisdom of No Escape* (Boston: Shambhala Publications, 1991).

5. Quoted in Matthew Fox, *The Coming of the Cosmic Christ* (San Francisco: HarperSanFrancisco, 1988), 56.

6. Quoted in Fox, *Coming of the Cosmic Christ*, 61.

7. T. S. Eliot, "East Coker," in *The Complete Poems and Plays: 1909–1950* (New York: Harcourt, Brace & World, 1952), 126–27.

8. Quoted in Fox, *Coming of the Cosmic Christ*, 222.

9. Matthew Fox, *Original Blessing* (Santa Fe, N.M.: Bear & Co., 1983), 135–36.

10. Ibid., 142.

11. Quoted in Fox, *Original Blessing*, 151.

12. Quoted in Fox, *Original Blessing*, 157.

13. Fox, *Original Blessing*, 159.

14. Ibid., 163.

15. Ibid., 175.

16. C. G. Jung, *Modern Man in Search of a Soul* (New York: Harcourt, Brace Jovanovich, 1933), 237.

17. Ibid., 235.

18. Marion Woodman, *The Pregnant Virgin* (Toronto: Inner City Books, 1985), 21–22.

19. Ibid., 10.

20. Quoted in Woodman, *Pregnant Virgin*, 121.

21. Mariann Burke, *Advent and Psychic Birth* (New York: Paulist Press, 1993), 99.

22. Ibid., 111.

23. Chödrön, *Wisdom of No Escape*, 91.

24. Ibid., 54.

25. Ibid., 91–92.

26. Thich Nhat Hanh, *Living Buddha, Living Christ* (New York: Riverhead Books, 1995), 124.

27. See, e.g., the stories about the Baba Yaga in Russia, Romania, Yugoslavia, and Poland.

28. Starhawk, *The Spiral Dance: The Rebirth of the Ancient Religion of the Goddess* (New York: Harper & Row, 1979), 94–95.

29. Singer-songwriter Colleen Fulmer has written a song called "Washerwoman God." See her collection *Cry of Ramah*, available from Sophia Spirit-Spirituality Resourses, West Hartford, Connecticut.

30. Marion Woodman with Jill Mellick, *Coming Home to Myself* (Berkeley, Calif.: Conari Press, 1998), 166.

31. Carol P. Christ, *Diving Deep and Surfacing: Women Writers on Spiritual Quest* (Boston: Beacon, 1980), 18–19.

32. *Meditations with Meister Eckhart* (ed. Matthew Fox; Santa Fe, N.M.: Bear & Co., 1983), 50.

33. Ibid., 41.

34. Ibid., 49.

35. Ibid., 51.

36. Kathryn Allen Rabuzzi, *The Sacred and the Feminine: Toward a Theology of Housework* (New York: Seabury, 1982), 32.

37. Naomi Goldenberg, *Changing of the Gods* (Boston: Beacon, 1979), 52.

38. Lauren Artress, *Walking a Sacred Path: Rediscovering the Labyrinth as a Spiritual Tool* (New York: Riverhead Books, 1995), 12.

39. Ibid., 182.

40. Ibid., 182–83.

41. See, e.g., Rom 5:12: "Sin came into the world through one man, and death came through sin, and so death spread to all because all have sinned." Cf. Rom 6:23: "The wages of sin is death."

42. Simone de Beauvoir, *The Second Sex* (trans. H. M. Parshley; London: Penguin, 1983), 177–78.

43. Rosemary Radford Ruether, "Motherearth and the Megamachine: A Theology of Liberation in a Feminine, Somatic, and Ecological Perspective," in *Womanspirit Rising* (ed. Carol P. Christ and Judith Plaskow; San Francisco: Harper Collins, 1992), 49.

44. Ibid., 48.

45. Rabbi Rami M. Shapiro, quoted in *Earth Prayers* (ed. Elizabeth Roberts and Elias Amidon; San Francisco: HarperSanFrancisco, 1991), 325.

46. Quoted in Roberts and Amidon, *Earth Prayers*, 227.

47. Erich Neumann, *The Great Mother* (trans. Ralph Manheim; Princeton, N.J.: Bollingen, 1974), 222.

48. John Houghton, *Murders and Mysteries, People and Plots: A Buckinghamshire, Bedfordshire, and Northamptonshire Miscellany* (Dunstable, U.K.: Book Castle, 1993), 104.

49. Quoted in *All in the End Is Harvest* (ed. Agnes Whitaker; London: Darton, Longman & Todd, 1984), 89.

50. Dorothee Sölle, "Paternalistic Religion as Experienced by Woman," in J.-B. Metz and E. Schillebeeckx Concilium 143, no. 3 (Edinburgh: T&T Clark, 1981), 73.

51. James Fowler, *Weaving a New Creation* (New York: HarperCollins, 1991), 111, 195.

52. Nhat Hanh, *Living Buddha, Living Christ*, 157.

CHAPTER 6
Ecofeminism: The Spiral of Life

The Spiral Dance

THE TEST OF ANY FAITH is its ability to connect the believer with others, with self, with the Divine, and with the world in ever deepening relationships of compassion and justice. "The soul is only as strong as its works," wrote Hildegard of Bingen (1098–1179). A faith or spirituality may be strong or comforting, challenging or inspiring, but unless it leads in the direction of healing and love beyond itself it is ultimately destructive. One of the critiques of the spiritualities that have emerged in the New Age, feminist, and other movements is that they can be inward looking and divorced from the needs and concerns of those outside the group. (The same, of course, may be said of more traditional perspectives, some of which are intensely introverted, with a shunning of "the world" beyond those who consider themselves and each other to be saved.) Vital and life-giving though the path of personal transformation and self-actualization may be, it is a circular path until it breaks beyond itself and begins the spiraling movement outward.

One day in April, early in my new work as a university campus minister, I took part in an Earth Day celebration that included a spiral dance from pagan traditions. The celebration had been organized by the campus Interfaith Council, which consisted of myself, the Jesuit and Christian Reformed campus ministers, a Hindu priest, a Muslim imam, a Jewish representative, and a Pagan. We had been meeting for several months in that particular configuration, and were slowly coming to understand and trust one another more. In particular the recent inclusion in the group of a Pagan, a woman who practiced the old religion of an earth-based spirituality, was a challenging development that had caused some discomfort and a great deal of healthy dialogue.

We had agreed to hold a celebration to mark Earth Day on a large green in the middle of the campus. Each of us contributed readings, prayers, music, or ritual from our own traditions, honoring the earth. With some thirty people in attendance, the Pagan member of our group led us in a spiral dance toward the end of the celebration. Up to that point we had been seated in a circle on the grass, quietly listening to the words, or singing. We had passed a bowl and pitcher of water around the circle and washed each others' hands in token of our desire to cease from harming the earth and to commit ourselves to healing and living more gently on it. When the dance began, a new level of opening to healing was set in motion. Joining hands, but with a break in the circle to enable the leader to begin making the spiral shape of the dance, we took the first self-conscious, tentative, laughing steps toward an opening up and a widening out that transforms. When I looked across the grass and saw one of my Christian colleagues, an older white male from a conservative denomination, holding hands with the younger female Pagan and dancing the prehistoric spiral dance of the Goddess, I knew I was seeing an extraordinary symbol of hope. More than that, it was almost a miracle, an event that would have been unthinkable a century or even fifty years before. It was barely thinkable the day it happened, but I remember it as an image of the uncoiling, freeing, connective energy that a holistic spiritual movement brings.

The spiral remains for me the shape and direction of a feminist faith. Such a faith is endlessly dynamic; it does not seek to contain or define itself with fixed creeds. It is outward moving in its quest for justice and healing transformation. It is connective, bringing together diversity and paradox not in a monolithic unity but in a web of relation, respect, and radical plurality. It ebbs and flows in a cyclic rhythm of action and meditation, knowledge and mystery, finding out and letting go. It is by nature holistic, with its roots in the ancient wisdom of Goddess worship, mysticism, aboriginal spirituality, and its branches reaching into liberation theology, interfaith ecumenism, and eco-spirituality. Living as we do in an era where world wars and the Cold War have been replaced by civil wars, very hot economic and cultural wars, and the global mutilation of our planet, this wisdom is needed as never before.

Domination and Ecocide

Ecofeminism, a word first used in 1974 by French author Francoise d'Eaubonne, goes beyond the ecological concerns of the Green movement and the social-gender concerns of the feminist movement by understanding that there is a deep and devastating link between the abuse of nature and the oppression of women. The same patriarchal forces that dominate women, children, and other humans considered lesser or weaker also dominate nature and the earth as subordinate resources to be controlled and exploited. Ecofeminist Julia Scofield Russell writes:

> It's becoming clear to us that women's liberation cannot be separated from the liberation of all—men, women, children, old, middle aged, Black, White, Yellow, Red, and mixed, rich and poor, animals, plants, and Mother Earth herself—from the tyranny of the conqueror society that now dominates the world. Whether it calls itself capitalistic, communistic, socialist, democratic, republican, multinational . . . is incidental to the primary characteristic they all share— the drive to conquest, the exploitation of women, nature, and each other.[1]

Similarly, ecofeminist author and activist Charlene Spretnak sees the fear and resentment that fuel patriarchy as giving rise to all forms of its culture of dominance, from the ecological destruction that is driving thousands of species into extinction every year, to the global militarism that consumes trillions of dollars annually on armaments while millions of infants die each year from starvation and disease.[2] A system based on power through exertion of control fears loss of that control and resents what cannot be tamed and brought to submission. The forces of nature, political enemies, and societal movements are all seen as threats to the power brokers of dominance, and so all are to be repressed like the shadow in the pysche.

In the introduction to her book *Gaia and God*, Rosemary Ruether writes that the quest of ecofeminism is for earth healing, whereby the broken relationships between men and women, between races, nations, and classes, and between the earth and humanity, can be made whole again. She adds, however, that "such a healing is possible only through recognition and transformation of the way in which Western culture, enshrined in part in Christianity, has justified such domination."[3]

Although Ruether has remained clearly within the Christian tradition, valuing and recovering its core commitment to justice and compassion, she also reveals what she calls the "toxic waste" of the Judeo-Christian tradition, in particular the way in which it has used theology to sanctify oppression and abuse. With a theology of creation that places God outside the universe as its maker, forming life either *ex nihilo* or from previously lifeless chaos, a fundamental split between the divine and the earthly entered the human mind and widened into a rampant dualism. The same creation theology saw man (not woman) as the pinnacle of creation and the center of the world, for whose use all other created things were given. So in Genesis we read that humanity alone is created "in the image of God" and charged with the divinely sanctioned duty to "fill the earth and subdue it; and have dominion over . . . every living thing that moves upon the earth" (Gen 1:27–28). While it is true that a theology of "enlightened guardianship" can develop from these texts, Ruether and others recognize that they have in fact been used to justify an abusive attitude to nature, seeing it as a resource to be exploited rather than the source of all life.

A theology of dominion names God as Lord, the supreme authority at the apex of a pyramid of power. Below God is the ruling-class male as God's authority on earth. (See Rom 13:1–7, where Paul expounds his understanding of earthly rulers as "instituted by God . . . to execute wrath on the wrongdoer.") A chain of command extends down to soulless, passive Nature, from which, as Christian theology drew on Greek Platonic thought, the human soul is destined to escape, going "home" to immortality in heaven. Thus, home is "somewhere else" with God, beyond this earth, and God is not revealed in Nature but is unknowable, except where he chooses to reveal himself in his sovereign freedom. Earth itself is merely a medium in which we exist until we "go home." It is not itself of value beyond its usefulness to us, and neither does it have the capacity for immortality. It is essentially expendable.

The apocalyptic hope of a dualistic theology involves the total and violent destruction of the earth. Christian fundamentalism preaches the literal end of the world at the second coming of Jesus—that is, at the return of Jesus to the world as an omnipotent ruler and judge, when the faithful will be "raptured," or taken bodily into heaven, and sinners will be punished in a hell on earth (see, e.g., Matt 24:36–44; Rev 14–16). In its contemporary form it contemplates global nuclear war as one vehicle for this expected end with escapist fatalism. Catherine Keller points to the connection between the degradation of the environment and the renewed interest in apocalyptic myths of the imminent end of the world: "Here is how the melodramatic voice of the connection sounds to me: 'Waste 'er! Go ahead, use 'er up! Devastate, consume, expend, squander, ravage, Daddy will give us a new one. The final rapture is almost here!'"[4]

The sin of a dominator theology is in its fruits: It sets up a hierarchy of power and exploitation; it splits humans from one another, from God, and from the earth; it operates through intimidation and enforcement; it is profoundly unjust and unbalanced. In his *Creation Spirituality*, an exploration of a spirituality that affirms creation as divine and inherently good, Matthew Fox sees the characteristics of an addictive personality in a society based on a dualistic, antinature, fundamentalist approach to religion: It exhibits a strong need to control, rather than an ability to relate in freedom and interdependence; it uses denial and dishonesty to support itself, refusing to see its destructiveness; and it is perfectionistic, inducing shame and demanding righteousness.[5] It is alienated within itself, and cannot be life giving. More than eight hundred years ago, Hildegard of Bingen wrote these words, which now seem prophetic:

> Humankind does well to keep honesty,
> to keep to truth.
> Those that love lies bring suffering
> not only to themselves but to others as well,
> since they are driven to ever more lies
> . . . .
> Now in the people that were meant to be green,

there is no more life of any kind.
There is only shrivelled barrenness.
The winds are burdened
by the utterly awful stink of evil,
selfish goings-on.
Thunderstorms menace.
The air belches out
the filthy uncleanliness of the peoples.
There pours forth an unnatural,
a loathsome darkness.
that withers the green,
and wizens the fruit
that was to serve as food for the people.
Sometimes this layer of air
is full,
full of a fog that is the source
of many destructive and barren creatures,
that destroy and damage the earth,
rendering it incapable
of sustaining humanity.
. . . . . .
The earth should not be injured.
The earth should not be destroyed.[6]

It is paradoxical that patriarchal theology, which is itself so quick to judge and condemn what is evil, can give rise to such appalling violence and destruction. It is too deeply flawed by its own inner disharmony to offer the healing this world so badly needs.

Paths to Healing

Ecofeminism seeks to heal the addictive dualisms that destroy life and stratify relationships. It identifies the fearfulness and escapism that lie behind patriarchal systems of exploitation, as well as the emptiness that gives rise to cultures of unsustainable greed. The problem is one of loss of connectedness, of amnesia. A culture that destroys its ecosystem and seeks to annihilate its enemies has forgotten that it is part of the whole; it is destroying itself. The ecofeminist voice names the connections that have been severed, and speaks of reweaving, of re-membering the dismembered world. It is engaged in a passionate, spiritual process that goes beyond theology and environmentalism to address a soul wound. As Carol Christ writes, "The crisis that threatens the destruction of the Earth is not only social, political, economic, and technological, but is at root spiritual."[7] Swimming against the tide of Christian fundamentalism, which looks for the second coming of Christ to judge the world and destroy all evil, with the violent imagery of the book of Revelation as its inspiration, ecofeminist theology speaks of the return to the religious imagination of Gaia.

The Second Coming of Gaia

If Gaia stands for an awareness of where humanity fits within creation, and a reverence for the earth, and a passionate love of the cycles of life, then we need her now more than ever. We need Gaia's voice, according to Ruether, to balance what has come to be understood as the voice of God, although they are barely even on speaking terms in Western religious thought and practice. We need heart, compassion, and love of life, as well as intellect, law, and organization. Ruether refuses to be co-opted by a counterdualism that sees Gaia, feminism, and women's wisdom as all-good, and that rejects God, traditional religion, and male leadership as totally negative. When she states that we need the "holy voices" of both Gaia and God, she is seeking the healing that comes from reintegration.

With the second coming of Gaia we return to our origins, both in the sense of returning to something of the outlook of our ancient ancestors who worshiped the Great Mother as symbol of all that is, and in the sense of remembering that we are not separate from nature, superior to it, or even in charge of it like stewards, but are part of it. As humans we differ from the rest of nature only in our capacity to be conscious, to be aware that we exist, and—most tragically—to become destructively alienated from our origins.

When Gaia is permitted to return—or, rather, when we return to Gaia—a healing humility becomes possible, dissolving the human arrogance which denies that we are latecomers to this planet, merely one very recent form of life in a vast story that stretches back beyond human imagination. Gaia reminds us (as the story of Adam's creation from the dust of the earth hints) that humans come from humus—the earth. To be human is to be of the earth, of the original humus, humble.

To honor Gaia is to learn to trust nature rather than dominate it, control it, or tame it. It is to have the humility to learn from nature, to study and imitate nature's cycles, diversity, and interdependence. Life on earth has evolved and sustained itself for billions of years, and now, with the power at our disposal to destroy all human life and much plant and animal life, we need to learn about survival. "We are to work *with* nature," writes Hildegard. "Without it we cannot survive."[8] Ruether describes the ways in which we can rebuild human society so as to live as sustaining members of the biotic communities on earth, rather than destroying those communities in arrogant ignorance.[9] And Fox describes the gifts of Wisdom that come from knowing the universe deeply. He names them as extravagance, interconnectivity, expansion, variety, creativity, emptiness (the ability to let go, to know creative solitude), justice, beauty, community, sacrifice, suffering and resurrection, paradox and humor, and work. These are not the vague, romanticized characteristics of nature that fill our fantasies as we dream of life in the country while trapped in the city: "They are virtues, sources of strength and empowerment . . . ways to serve the universe."[10] They are a far cry from the imperative to "subdue the earth."

From the perspective of a theology that sees God as primarily transcendent, as essentially separate from creation, it is easy to ignore the voice of Gaia, to dismiss her wisdom as irrelevant, to consider the earth disposable. But as we are beginning to realize the damage this has done, those who care about the earth are finding their images of God softening, as Gaia draws closer, appearing in surprising places. Churches are starting to hold St. Francis Day celebrations, animal blessings, Earth Day liturgies and Environmental Sabbaths. Outdoor worship services are becoming more common. Wiccans and other Pagans dialogue and work with Jews and Christians. God is described in one contemporary and increasingly popular version of the Lord's Prayer as "Earth-maker, Pain-bearer, Life-giver, Source of all that is and that shall be, Father and Mother of us all."[11] Gaia is, it seems, on speaking terms with God.

Panentheism, the teaching that God is in all things, being both immanent and transcendent, is becoming not a marginal piece of theology of dubious orthodoxy, but the stated belief of mainstream Christian theologians and laypeople.[12] An extract from author Alice Walker's *The Color Purple* is frequently quoted to illustrate the move from theism to panentheism, from God to Gaia, in an accessible, almost anecdotal way. One character, Shug, a vibrant woman of color, is describing to the younger, less confident woman Celie how her image of God changed:

> My first step from the old white man was trees. Then air. Then birds. Then other peoples. But one day when I was sitting quiet and feeling like a motherless child, which I was, it come to me: that feeling of being part of everything, not separate at all. I knew that if I cut a tree my arm would bleed. And I laughed and I cried and I ran all around the house. I knew just what it was. . . . I think it pisses God off if you walk by the color purple in a field and don't notice it. . . . Everything want to be loved.[13]

Nature-based spiritualities such as Wicca are centered on the belief that the earth is sacred ("Everything want to be loved"), and humans are part of that mysterious, living, dying, regenerating whole. So Starhawk describes Wicca as a religion of ecology, and the Goddess as All-That-Is-One, earth, air, fire, water, and spirit. She is divine and yet immanent in the world and manifested in nature. It is then precisely because the Divine is found within the earthy and natural that earth and nature are treated with respect and reverence.

This is not so different from the mystic insight that creation is a "mirror of God that glistens and glitters," in Hildegard's words, revealing the Creator to us within it: "As human persons view creation with compassion, in trust, they see the Lord. It is God which humankind is then able to recognize in every living thing."[14] Compassion and trust are necessary in order that we see creation as more than a resource or object. Ruether refers to an attitude that sees and accepts the "thouness" of nonhuman forms of life, and refuses to treat them as mere "things," available simply for human use. She believes that this attitude is vital if human and other forms of life on this planet are to survive; it is ethical, since there is a "covenantal relation between humans and all other life forms, as one family united by one source of life"; and it is theologically grounded once the anthropocentric God up in heaven has given way to the Divine who is present both within and beyond the complex web of all life.

Homecoming-Homemaking

There is a sense of coming home in a spirituality that is rooted in the earth. The dualistic striving to "get to heaven" is replaced by a deep awareness that we are already at home, and we need go nowhere else to find God. The Greek word *oikos*, from which "ecology" is derived, means "home"; we are learning to be at home again in our bodies, in our earthy existence, in this universe, with our companion beings who share home with us. We do not need to mortify our bodies, shun the world, tame nature, or subdue the earth; we simply need to come home, and to make our home *with* the earth, not just *on* it.

The homemaking metaphor has been used by Katherine Zappone, a feminist theologian, as an intentional reclamation of a lowly, diminished image of women's work.[15] As a metaphor for restoring a healthy earth-human relationship she finds it both hopeful and creative, because it begins not with humanity as central and supreme, but with earth as our context and sustaining medium. It is biocentric, going beyond the concepts of stewardship or "earth-keeping," and it acknowledges that all species, nonhuman and human, belong interdependently in this home. The task of homemaking, clearing up our toxicity, and healing the wounds humans have inflicted on other species and on each other is the task not only of women as supposedly closer to nature, but of all humanity.

As we grow to understand and love the earth more, so our desire to cease from harming it will grow. It is not necessary to believe in a divine imperative coming from outside to tell us to save the earth; it is not necessary to believe in a personal Gaia or Goddess who weeps as we damage her body the earth. We simply have to love the earth enough to stop the destruction, and that means understanding that the earth is our home, not a bus stop along the way. With considerable honesty, Carol Christ writes:

I imagine, but I do not know, that the universe has an intelligence, a Great Spirit, that it cares as we care. I imagine that all that is cares. Sometimes I feel that I hear the universe weeping or laughing, speaking to me. But I do not know. What I do know is that whether the universe has a centre of consciousness or not, the sight of a field of flowers in the color purple, the rainbow, must be enough to stop us from destroying all that is and wants to be.[16]

When we know that this earth is truly our home, then salvation is no longer an act in an apocalyptic future, but is healing and liberation here and now. "We need no new heaven and Earth," writes Catherine Keller. "We have this Earth, this sky, this water to renew."[17] Sometimes, in fact, we simply have to step out of the way and let the earth save *us*, by teaching us its wisdom and schooling us in its ways. "Save the Humans" reads a whale-shaped bumper sticker on my friends' car. *We* are the species who has forgotten who it is and where it belongs.

Judaism has a strong tradition of calling for right relationships on earth between people and species, based on a right relationship with God. The prophets envisioned "new heavens and a new earth" resulting from transformation of the old and restoration of justice, not in a paradisial future after the destruction of the world. The words of Isaiah, for example, are decidedly earthy; his vision is of peace for this world, not in an otherworldly spiritual realm:

> For I am about to create new heavens
>   and a new earth.
>
> I will rejoice in Jerusalem. . . .
>
> no more shall the sound of weeping be heard in it,
>   or the cry of distress.
> No more shall there be in it
>   an infant that lives but a few days,
>   or an old person who does not live out a lifetime. . . .
>
> They shall build houses and inhabit them;
>   they shall plant vineyards and eat their fruit. . . .
>
> The wolf and the lamb shall feed together,
>   the lion shall eat straw like the ox. . . .
>
> They shall not hurt or destroy
>   on all my holy mountain,
>   says the LORD. (Isa 65:17, 19–21, 25)

By contrast, Christianity has often spiritualized the vision of a better future, so that Jerusalem becomes "the new Jerusalem," descending from heaven, with angels at its gates, walls of jasper, buildings and streets of gold, gates of pearl, and jewels adorning its foundations (see Rev 21). This is not a vision of earth as our home, restored and healed; it is a complete celestial makeover after global destruction, some time in the future.

Yet Jesus' message of the coming of the "kingdom of heaven" or "kingdom of God" seems originally to have referred to a new way of being, seeing, and relating *now*. Although it too has been spiritualized by a dualistic theology and equated with an apocalyptic day of judgment or day of Jesus' return in power and glory (an image which brings to mind the warrior invasions of Old Europe), the gospels of Matthew, Mark, and Luke suggest that Jesus saw "the kingdom" as a present possibility. He often used images from nature to describe it: Like yeast mixed into flour, or a tiny seed that will become a large plant, it is not always evident, yet it has the potential to bring about transformation (see Mark 4:26–32; Matt 13:33). It can be entered into in the present, or be seen to be near (see, e.g., Luke 10:11; Matt 23:13). When Jesus healed a man on one occasion, he declared that the kingdom had come (Luke 11:20). Most significantly, when asked when the kingdom would come, his reply was that it is not an external event that can be located, but is an inner, present reality: "The kingdom of God is not coming with things that can be observed; nor will they say, 'Look, here it is!' or 'There it is!' For, in fact, the kingdom of God is within [or "among"] you" (Luke 17:20–21).

In accord with this nonfuturistic understanding of heaven, one version of the Lord's Prayer, as indicated in a footnote in the NRSV, has in place of the familiar "Your kingdom come" the words "Your Holy Spirit come upon us and cleanse us" (Luke 11:2). Heaven on earth in Jesus' teaching is not a postapocalyptic hope, but a reality made possible by profound inner transformation through the Holy Spirit in the present.

If heaven is not viewed spatially or temporally as somewhere else and as some-time in the future, then heaven and earth are not perceived as opposites, and we need not flee one to escape to the other. In fact the converse is true: In order to experience heaven we need to enter more deeply into the earth as our home, and work for the healing and transformation of ourselves, one another, and all of creation through the creative breath of the Spirit. Otherworldly fantasies and miracles are not necessary. As Thich Nhat Hanh writes:

> Our true home is in the present moment. The miracle is not to walk on water. The miracle is to walk on the green earth in the present moment. Peace is all around us—in the world and in nature—and within us—in our bodies and our spirits. Once we learn to touch this peace, we will be healed and transformed. It is not a matter of faith; it is a matter of practice.[18]

Coming home means finding heaven on earth, the sacred in the earthy, God in our midst. Celtic spirituality is becoming more well-known and widely explored today in part because it has been recognized as maintaining this integrating perspective, and resisting the pull to split heaven from earth. Like its complex and beautiful interwoven designs depicting birds and beasts, it weaves together the divine and the earthy because it sees the divine *in* the earthy. The daily prayers of Scottish Highlanders were spoken with eyes open in the midst of the chores and routines of life—while kindling a fire, milking a cow, cutting peat, rowing a boat. God was at home with the Highlanders. It was not necessary to go into a church building and to kneel down and close one's eyes to find God in prayer, because God was "under my roof," "upon my doorstep," "between thy two shoulders," "in my steps." All of nature was experienced as "full of His blessing." There was nowhere that God was not, and body and soul were understood to be intimately linked, not striving against each other.

Thus Esther de Waal, historian and Christian author, writes of the Celtic people: "[They] found it entirely natural to see God in every moment and at every level of their ordinary life. . . . The material things of daily life almost inevitably became a way to God for a people who always speak of body and soul with equal respect and for whom the borderline of secular and sacred seems irrelevant."[19]

Contempt for the body and distrust of the world characterize a theology of alienation. Much of the oppressive desire to control therefore springs from fear and distaste. By contrast, a spirituality of being at home in our bodies and on the earth fosters trust, respect, and a celebration of sensuality. "There is nothing in the universe as sensuous as God," says contemporary Celtic author John O'Donohue.[20] The tangible, aesthetic, physical realm can be a revelation of the Divine as much as the invisible, ascetic, and spiritual, although much of Western theology elevates the latter and rejects the former. Sensuality, indeed, used to be the word for the "sin" of loving the world too much. But Eckhart, who describes God as "voluptuous and delicious,"[21] teaches a way to find God within the stuff of life: "Spirituality is not to be learned by flight from the world, by running away from things, or by turning solitary and going apart from the world. Rather . . . we must learn to penetrate things and find God there."[22]

Women have been both overidentified with our bodies (as though men are somehow less physical) and at the same time denigrated along with physicality as unholy. In the Christian tradition a hostility to bodiliness has been evident in prohibitions against nudity, obligatory celibacy for priests and members of religious orders, restrictions against menstruating women setting foot within the church sanctuary, and restriction of sexual acts to the intended purpose of procreation. Such attitudes have been harmful both to women and to men, creating an inner split between body and soul that is artificial and destructive. The idea that the body is "the angel of the soul" or "the mirror of the soul," a beautiful sacrament that allows the soul to become visible,[23] has been lost to many, who have instead ingested a diet of shame, discomfort, and alienation with regard to the body.

Matthew Fox advocates a celebration of sensuality as one way to return home to the body as holy.[24] Sensual experiences, he points out, have a way of making us participants in life and its natural processes, not commanders exerting control over them. He lists as sensual such experiences as walking barefoot, making love, dancing, smelling lilacs, crying, making or listening to music, hugging a baby, getting a back rub, being alive and aware of being alive. Immersion in the physical world need not mean surrendering indiscriminately to any bodily appetite or dulling the life of the spirit. Rather, it can be part of a deeply spiritual process of coming back home to ourselves, to each other, to this world of which we are a part, in profound awareness and gratitude.

Thich Nhat Hanh tells the story of a person who asked the Buddha, "Sir, what do you and your monks practice?" The Buddha replied, "We sit, we walk, and we eat." When the questioner objected that everyone sits, walks, and eats, the Buddha answered, "When we sit, we *know* we are sitting. When we walk, we *know* we are walking. When we eat, we *know* we are eating."[25]

Thus, a walk can be a prayer, a drink of tea a sacrament, a dance an embodied liturgy. Slowly, as this wisdom enters mainstream Christianity (often through women's initiatives), the cerebral worship of Protestantism and the congregationally passive rites of Catholicism are becoming balanced with drama, dance, the involvement of children, the intentional use of color, sound, and silence, and the honoring of the four directions, elements, or seasons. Ritual is used consciously, not mechanically, with creativity and imagination, to concretize or embody truths we need to touch in times of transition, loss, or celebration. Christianity, as a faith based on the concept of incarnation, "Wisdom enfleshed in Jesus,"[26] badly needs to recover its trust in the body and respect for physicality. It may then be possible to move beyond the fearfulness that leads to fundamentalism, and to a stance of awe at the complexities and mysteries of the world, which is our sacred home. As Catherine Keller states, echoing Jesus' words, "Anxiety is healed not by elimination of complexity but by the cosmic trust of the lilies."[27]

Reweaving

Like liberation theology, the ecofeminist path is by nature activist. The vision of a healed world calls for engagement in the process of making that possible, in the face of the widespread cynicism or despair that views the destructive end of the world as inevitable. The process, however, goes far beyond such "Band-Aid" approaches as more recycling or fewer emissions of greenhouse gases; rather, a transformation of the entire fabric of relationships of domination is necessary. "We cannot graft peace and ecological balance on a dominator system," writes Riane Eisler.

"A just and egalitarian society is impossible without the full and equal partnership of men and women."[28] And this partnership must extend to people of every culture and status, as well as to nonhuman species. All are affected by the present patterns of domination and exploitation, so all are involved in the reweaving. Starhawk explains how the issues are interconnected:

> Environmental issues *are* social justice issues, for it is the poor who are forced to work directly with unsafe chemicals, in whose neighborhoods toxic waste incinerators are planned, who cannot afford to buy bottled water and organic vegetables or pay for medical care. Environmental issues are international issues, for we cannot simply export unsafe pesticides, toxic wastes, and destructive technologies without poisoning the whole living body of the Earth.[29]

Once we understand deeply that the whole earth is our home, and all its inhabitants our family, then the "not in my backyard" mentality expands to the knowledge that *no* place is acceptable for dumping toxic waste, testing nuclear weapons, harvesting to extinction, "cleansing" for ethnic purity. The worldview of global partnership in the complex web of life leads to an ethic of widening responsibility whereby one species cannot poison another, one nation cannot sell land mines to another, one sector of society cannot economically enslave another. Albert Einstein spoke of our need to widen the circle of compassion, to infuse our biological connectedness with a connection of mutual care, so that not only do we acknowledge that all of life springs from one source, reaching back to the origins of the cosmos, but we also learn to live with empathy and concern beyond our narrow self-interest. In this we can learn from nature, which sustains itself through a delicate balance of interdependence. As Fox observes, the human quest for compassion and justice-making is simply our part in the dance of all creation for balance.[30]

Fox's four paths of creation spirituality outline ways in which reweaving the world becomes possible. On the *via positiva* we fall in love with all of creation, so that we no longer take it for granted but delight in it, stand in awe of it, seek to know it more deeply. On the *via negativa* we allow our hearts to be broken in order for compassion to flow; we see the woundedness of the world, and we grieve for it; we do not turn away in numbness or despair, but love enough to feel the pain. On the *via creativa* we develop imaginative, passionate ways in which to cocreate with the Divine, taking seriously our ability to birth ideas, become conscious, and affect life on this planet for good or ill. The *via transformativa*, finally, brings together celebration and justice as we work to relieve suffering, find balance, and live lives of wide compassion. This way calls for "prophetic interference," as visionaries such as ecofeminists, creation theologians, and mystics cry out for an all-embracing justice that will bring healing and peace. As Hildegard wrote:

Good people, . . . God hugs you. You are encircled by the arms of the mystery of God. . . . Humankind full of all creative possibilities is God's work. Humankind alone is called to assist God. Humankind is called to co-create. . . . With nature's help, humankind can set into creation all that is necessary and life-sustaining. . . . This is possible through the right and holy utilization of the earth, the earth in which humankind has its source. The sum total of heaven and earth, everything in nature, is thus won to use and purpose.[31]

"This is possible." We need to hear that, repeatedly, to be saved from falling into hopelessness. Ecofeminists suggest that activism be rooted always in community, so that the efforts of individuals are supported by a greater whole, and are thus sustainable. "How do we carry on a struggle to heal the world and to build a new biospheric community in the face of this intransigent system of death?" asks Ruether. "It is my belief that those who want to carry on this struggle in a sustained way must build strong base communities of celebration and resistance."[32] Against the prevalent cultures of dominance and deceit, she calls for the creation of cultures of critique and compassion. Beginning with ourselves, but in small groups of those who share global concerns, we must start the process of *metanoia*, of deep turning around and away from destructive lifestyles, politics, and theologies. We must challenge the thinking and practice that make human poverty and war seem inevitable, and earth's degradation a necessary evil. From base communities we can create a mental and spiritual climate that makes it possible to dream, create, invent, lobby, organize, and activate for a better world. Together, in local and global partnerships, we can cocreate the kingdom of heaven (or kinship of God) on earth.

This is radically alternative; it challenges what has been established as the status quo for many centuries. It can seem an impossibly huge undertaking. What we need, according to Ruether, "is neither optimism nor pessimism . . . but committed love. This means that we remain committed to a vision and to concrete communities of life no matter what the 'trends' may be."[33]

Starhawk also stresses the need for community, both as a reality which emerges once we understand that, in Hildegard's words, "all things are penetrated with connectedness," so that we overcome our alienation from others, and as a place for empowerment and activism. She refutes the assumption of Christian fundamentalism, which sees the goal of faith as individual salvation, and says that the goal of an earth-based spirituality is the creation of a community in which relationships with the earth and all its species are restored. It is no coincidence that such fundamentalism typically has little to say about injustice, environmental concerns, and global cultures of warfare and oppression other than to see them as caused by "the enemy," Satan, or anyone else other than God's elect, since it is rooted in a theology of dualism and alienation, and it is not at home on the earth. In Chung Hyun Kyung's word, it "otherizes" those who are different. It cannot integrate and heal, because it lacks compassion, the ability to feel with another as though the other were oneself.

The fundamentalist or dualist in all of us makes it possible for us to send our armies to kill "the enemy" because they are not "us," or to eat food from factory farms because we did not have to see the animals' inhumane living and dying. It makes it possible for us to enjoy affluent, consumerist lifestyles because the poor are not there to beseech us to share; they are elsewhere, voiceless, and rendered invisible by the touch of a television control button.

The gospel of Jesus calls us to love our neighbor as we love ourselves, not to otherize, split, and distance ourselves from our neighbor. And who is our neighbor? Every living being with which we share this planet, for we are all children of the one Great Spirit—perhaps especially, according to the parable of the Good Samaritan, those who are least like us, those we tend to look down on or ignore. When we are challenged to "be perfect," as God is perfect (Matt 5:48), we understand that the deeper meaning of this is to "be compassionate," as Luke wrote (Luke 6:36), or to "be all-embracing," as the original sense of the word might have been—to live with a heart opened wide to inclusiveness and justice, as we become conscious that "our own pulse beats in every stranger's throat . . . and . . . we can hear it in water, in wood, and even in stone."[34]

Experiments in Faith

My departure from parish ministry freed me to be bolder in how I practiced and shared my faith. I delighted in being no longer narrowly defined as Anglican, but as ecumenical—a word derived from the Greek, meaning "for the whole world." Sometimes I jokingly referred to myself as the "no-name brand" chaplain, since religious brand loyalty has been one of the most destructive forces on earth. Funded by three denominations but serving the university population as a whole, I was especially concerned to reach those outside the church who had no articulated faith.

At the same time, as parents of three preschool-age children, David and I arrived in our new community wanting to be able to continue sharing both ministry and parenting in ways that would be healthy for us, our children, the university, and society. We were eager to join with others who were doing things differently, such as choosing to live on one salary, breaking down the usual gender roles at home, and addressing the issues of justice at work. We wanted to live and work in what Thich Nhat Hanh calls "a mini pure land," a small outpost of the kinship of God, where a faith community could put its vision into practice while challenging and supporting each other.

Working outside the usual parameters set by church and society, I have been able to live in various experiments of faith. In my university ministry I have been a leader or participant in groups worshiping the Feminine Divine, studying the goddess cultures of the past, working for gay, lesbian, bisexual, and transgendered rights, revising traditional liturgy to be inclusive of minorities and sensitive to women's perspectives, reading feminist and ecofeminist books, coordinating inter-faith presentations and dialogues, working for peace and social justice, and orga-nizing for environmental activism. As students, faculty, and staff together, almost always in small groups operating with informality and consensus, we have prayed, read, laughed, danced, cried, protested, argued, raged, meditated, run dry, and been revitalized together. My partners in it have included Pagans and Catholics, Hindus and Jews, Buddhists and Muslims. They have been born-again Christians and Marxists, feminists and conservatives, queer and straight, people of color and WASPS—all sorts and conditions of people, with a vast variety of backgrounds and passions.

In parallel, our family became part of an intentional ecumenical Christian community for three years, meeting five times a week to pray together in the early morning, once a week for a communal meal, and every Sunday evening for wor-ship. We were a community of families, couples, and individuals, from infants to the late middle-aged, numbering fifteen, and sharing our resources while living in separate houses. We called ourselves the Community of New Justice, and talked of eventually living in community, in harmony with the land, in relationships of respect and interdependence. Although the group lacked the stability and cohesion to stay together, it was a powerful experience of breaking through the usual walls of the nuclear family or the generational divides, and of catching the excitement of incarnating something of the gospel call to radical living.

In ministry and in family life, the experiences have been kaleidoscopic in their shifting, fragmentary, colorful reality. They have rarely been neat and sorted, but the chaos and challenge of new ways of being, new connections, and new relationships have forced me to let go of security and fall into creativity. Kaleidoscope, labyrinth, spiral, and web are all metaphors of change and movement, complexity and growth, and they are essential to my understanding of the journey of faith. From my teenage vocation to priesthood, to my hesitant exploration of the Feminine Divine, to my ministry in Québec and northern Ontario and now on a university campus, the path has been one of letting go, opening up, going deeper, living more boldly. A prayer from *The Book of Alternative Services of the Anglican Church of Canada*, says, "Strengthen us in the risk of faith." Hildegard urges us to have "greening power," and to be moist and verdant. Faith is about risk, growth, and life. It affects every aspect of our lives, and is constantly ready to surprise us with where it leads.

One evening at the university, Starhawk and Donna Read visited to present a preview of Starhawk's novel *The Fifth Sacred Thing*[35], in which she conveys her spir-ituality and politics in the form of a story, and Donna Read's film *Full Circle*, which completed the National Film Board trilogy on women's spirituality. The event began with a woman dancing with snakes entwined around her arms, as dancers to the Goddess performed in ancient cultures. I leaned across to a colleague and whispered that I hoped our bishops would never hear of this! It felt like feasting on forbidden fruit and finding it miraculously nourishing. The evening continued with the screening of the film and a reading from the novel. Although organized at short notice with mainly word of mouth publicity, the room was packed with more than two hundred people, mostly women. The atmosphere was informal but intense, as we saw images and heard words that have been missing from our religious consciousness for so long.

At the end, Starhawk led us in a chant. Too crowded to form a spiral and dance, we held hands as we stood in rows, and sang to a drumming rhythm over and over again, "She changes everything she touches, and everything she touches changes." The Feminine Divine, Goddess, Sophia, God as Mother and Spirit of Life—whatever we name her—changes our androcentric theology, our relationships of domination and control, our view of ourselves, our place in the cosmos. She pushes us where we get stuck, connects us where we are separated, dares us when we want to play safe. She blows where she wills (John 3:8), makes dry bones live (Ezek 37:5), comes as the kiss between justice and peace (Ps 85:10), and breathes courage and passion into her people (Acts 2:1–4). She is green and juicy—a warm, moist, salty God.[36] Without her, we cannot be healed or save our world.

Notes

1. Julia Scofield Russell, "The Evolution of an Ecofeminist," in *Reweaving the World: The Emergence of Ecofeminism* (ed. Irene Diamond and Gloria Feman Orenstein; San Francisco: Sierra Club Books, 1990), 225.

2. Charlene Spretnak, "Ecofeminism: Our Roots and Flowering," in Diamond and Orenstein, *Reweaving the World*, 5.

3. Rosemary Radford Ruether, *Gaia and God* (San Francisco: HarperSanFrancisco, 1992), 1.

4. Catherine Keller, "Women Against Wasting the World," in Diamond and Orenstein, *Reweaving the World*, 250.

5. Matthew Fox, *Creation Spirituality* (San Francisco: HarperSanFrancisco, 1991).

6. Gabriele Uhlein, ed., *Meditations with Hildegard of Bingen* (Santa Fe, N.M.: Bear and Co., 1983), 76–78.

7. Carol Christ, "Rethinking Theology and Nature," in Diamond and Orenstein, *Reweaving the World*, 58.

8. Uhlein, *Meditations with Hildegard of Bingen*, 71 (emphasis mine).

9. Ruether, *Gaia and God*, 258–68.

10. Fox, *Creation Spirituality*, 43–54.

11. See, e.g., *A New Zealand Prayer Book* (Auckland: Collins, 1989), 181.

12. See, e.g., Marcus Borg, *The God We Never Knew* (San Francisco: HarperSanFrancisco, 1997), 32–51.

13. Alice Walker, *The Color Purple* (New York: Pocket Books, 1982), 178–79.

14. Uhlein, *Meditations with Hildegard of Bingen*, 91.

15. Katherine Zappone, *The Hope for Wholeness: A Spirituality for Feminists* (Mystic, Conn.: Twenty-Third Publications, 1991), 113–45.

16. Christ, "Rethinking Theology and Nature," 69.

17. Keller, "Women Against Wasting the World," 263.

18. Thich Nhat Hanh, *Living Buddha, Living Christ* (New York: Riverhead Books, 1995), 23–24.

19. Esther de Waal, *God under My Roof* (Oxford: SLG Press, 1984), 2.

20. John O'Donohue, *Anam Cara* (New York: HarperCollins, 1998), 50.

21. *Meditations with Meister Eckhart* (ed. Matthew Fox; Santa Fe, N.M.: Bear and Co., 1983), 33.

22. Ibid., 90.

23. See O'Donohue, *Anam Cara*, 44–50.

24. See Matthew Fox, *Whee! We, Wee All the Way Home* (Gaithersburg, Md.: Consortium Books, 1976).

25. Nhat Hanh, *Living Buddha, Living Christ*, 14.

26. From Colleen Fulmer's song "Ruah," in *Cry of Ramah* (cassette) (Cincinnati: St. Anthony Messenger, 1985).

27. Keller, "Women Against Wasting the World," 260.

28. Riane Eisler, "The Gaia Tradition and the Partnership Future," in Diamond and Orenstein, *Reweaving the World*, 34.

29. Starhawk, "Power, Authority, and Mystery," in Diamond and Orenstein, *Reweaving the World*, 82–83.

30. Fox, *Creation Spirituality*, 23.

31. Uhlein, *Meditations with Hildegard of Bingen*, 90, 106–7.

32. Ruether, *Gaia and God*, 268–69.

33. Ibid., 273.

34. Barbara Deming, in Elizabeth Roberts and Elias Amidon, eds., *Earth Prayers* (San Francisco: HarperSanFrancisco, 1991), 77.

35. Starhawk, *The Fifth Sacred Thing* (New York: Bantam, 1993).

36. See Edwina Gateley, *A Warm, Moist, Salty God: Women Journeying towards Wisdom* (Trabuco Canyon, Calif.: Source Books, 1993).

CHAPTER 7
Interfaith: Widening the Circle of Wisdom

Christian Exclusivism and Feminism

THE CLAIM THAT SALVATION comes only through faith in Jesus Christ is central to traditional Christianity and is certainly expressed in the Bible. The most frequently quoted verses that support this view are the following, none of which seems open to debate:

> I [Jesus] am the way, and the truth, and the life. No one comes to the Father except through me. (John 14:6)

> There is salvation in no one else [but Jesus], for there is no other name under heaven given among mortals by which we must be saved. (Acts 4:12)

> For there is one God;
> there is also one mediator between God and humankind,
> Christ Jesus, himself human,
> who gave himself a ransom for all. (1 Tim 2:5–6)

The uniqueness of Jesus Christ and the exclusivity of Christianity go hand in hand. When Jesus is seen not as one religious leader or spiritual teacher among many (as Islam, for instance, sees him), but as the only incarnation of God on earth, and the only one capable of procuring salvation by his sacrificial death, then Christianity, as the only religion that proclaims this, is the only true religion. From this perspective, other faiths may have their merits, but since they do not proclaim Christ as Savior and Lord they are all to a greater or lesser extent misguided, false, or deceitful.

Christian exclusivism has always made me queasy. Long before I had the theological vocabulary to understand and challenge it I knew at a gut level that it did not come from the God I loved. One inescapable conclusion of an exclusivist position was that my father, the adamant agnostic and humanitarian who could not accept Christianity as his personal faith, was destined for hell, or, at the very least, could not be certain of salvation. I know this was a cause of considerable anxiety for my mother, who once told me that she took great comfort from Paul's statement that "the unbelieving husband is made holy through his wife" (1 Cor 7:14). Presumably, as two people united in marriage had become "one flesh," the faith of one was deemed sufficient for both. She had, in other words, found a loophole. But the fundamental premise remained that unbelievers were not saved, and I could not stomach it.

My conservative evangelical friends accused me of picking and choosing from the Bible and from Christian teaching the parts I liked, while rejecting the uncomfortable parts. I felt duly reprimanded, though I continued to be selective. Now I interpret the tension differently: It is not a disagreement between conservatives and liberals, between Bible-believing Christians and Christians lost in the murky soup of relativism; rather, it is at root a difference in the way we understand God. A God who damns non-Christians is simply too small, too mean-spirited. A God who does not love my father at least as much as I do is not worth worshiping.

From a feminist perspective, Christian exclusivism is yet one more fruit from the tree of patriarchy that insists on dividing the world into Us and Them, in this case into the saved and the unsaved. Feminist spirituality, by contrast, begins with an assumption of God's inclusive, unconditional love for all, and knows that "perfect love casts out fear" (1 John 4:18). It rejects the violent logic of punishment, hellfire, and damnation. As Julian of Norwich knew, God's wisdom, love, and unity "do not allow Him to be angry," and between God and our souls "there is neither wrath nor forgiveness" because nothing can come between us.[1]

What God has done and revealed in Jesus is a sign of God's abundant, unrestricted, ubiquitous, and generous grace, not a boundary on it. The incarnation, crucifixion, and resurrection of Jesus tell of God's costly involvement in this messy, broken world, and of God's astounding gift of new life through, in, and beyond death. This gospel is always and everywhere true; there is no time or place where God is not with us, healing, forgiving, liberating, transforming. God is a universalist; it is we who have made God parochial and salvation sectarian.

But the history of Christian exclusivism tells another story. Believing themselves to have been entrusted with a divine commission to convert all nations to Christianity (Matt 28:19), and to do so in order to bring about the end of the old world and inaugurate a new age of peace under the rulership of Christ (Matt 24:14; Mark 13:10), missionaries from the very earliest years of the church undertook perilous journeys and endured extreme adversity in order to carry out this task. The spread of the gospel, however, was more akin to the spread of a plague when it was linked with violence and intolerance. The virus of patriarchy can turn good news into deadly news, and Jesus of Nazareth then begins to acquire the attributes of the God of early Israel, who commanded the wholesale destruction of the worshipers of other gods.

When Christianity was established as the official religion of the Roman Empire in the fourth century, the religious-political system called Christendom was born. Secular power was wedded to sacred authority, and mission became in part a military operation. The Crusades of the eleventh to fourteenth centuries were waged against non-Christians, "heretical" Christians, and political opponents, in bloody battles for control of land and orthodoxy. Massacres and other atrocities were committed by the Crusaders in the name of the gospel and of Christ, with full support of the church hierarchy. Today the word "crusade" retains connotations of extremist activism, and it is little wonder that the North American student Christian group Campus Crusade for Christ is regarded with deep suspicion by Jewish and Muslim groups on campuses.

Each era of Christendom has had its own shameful history of violence and intolerance. In the medieval centuries, those tortured and killed as witches were the victims; during the colonization of the "New World," the native peoples of the Americas suffered cultural genocide as they were killed, forcibly converted, and removed from their ancestral homes; the slave trade based in Africa was long upheld by Christian nations as a morally acceptable way in which to civilize the "heathen"; and in Canada, as elsewhere, residential schools were established by the churches and government in order to educate the native children in the language, faith, and culture of Europeans, while at the same time systematically erasing native spirituality, culture, and pride with abusive arrogance.

I do not doubt the sincerity and commitment of many missionaries any more than I doubt the courage and loyalty of many in the armed forces. But the ideology of domination underlies this exclusivist theology of mission as surely as it underlies the politics of warfare. The "Great Commission" of Matthew's gospel is couched in the language of authority and obedience, which has more in common with the world of hierarchical power structures than with Christ's vision of a community of servanthood and mutual love:

> And Jesus came and said to them [i.e., eleven of the male disciples], "*All authority* in heaven and on earth has been given to me. Go therefore and make disciples of all nations, baptizing them in the name of the Father and of the Son and of the Holy Spirit, and teaching them to *obey* everything that I have *commanded* you." (Matt 28:18-20; emphasis mine)

Feminist theologians have pointed to the links between the language of mission and that of militarism: Groups are "targeted" for evangelism; air forces conduct bombing "missions"; Christian hymnody includes such well-known songs as "Onward Christian Soldiers." Indeed, the Salvation Army has based its entire metaphor for ministry on a military model. Similarly, in sexual language the position for intercourse nicknamed "the missionary position" involves the male lying on top of the female and penetrating an implicitly passive partner. Mary Daly denounces the Christian concept of mission as inherently phallic and violent, whereby God "thrusts his will upon others" from outside and by force if necessary.[2] Asian feminist theologian Chung Hyun Kyung describes much missionary activity as fascist and imperialist, destructively interwoven with the colonialism that has raped her country.[3]

Assumptions and Accusations

Underlying the Christian theology of mission as it has been traditionally understood are various key assumptions, not all of which are made explicit, but all of which have the inevitable consequences of exclusivism and intolerance:

> Christians have something that non-Christians do not, namely, salvation and a right knowledge of God.
>
> Christians therefore have a superior culture and society, whose mores and structures should be brought to bear on other cultures.
>
> Non-Christian faiths have nothing of essential value to teach Christians.
>
> Sin is the primary human problem, not ignorance, fear, or desire, and therefore salvation through Christ is the only solution, not enlightenment.
>
> Repentance and an articulated faith in Christ is a prerequisite for salvation.
>
> Right belief is more important than right action.
>
> Eternal damnation or separation from God awaits those outside salvation; thus, proselytizing is urgently important and the use of any means is justified.
>
> Heaven is for Christians only.
>
> God's grace (rather like the bounty of the World Bank) is given only under certain conditions to those who fit the appropriate category, and non-Christians do not qualify.
>
> God has only one plan of salvation, one path to heaven. There is no other way.

Liberal theology, with its demythologizing of heaven and hell, has distanced itself from these assumptions. Mission as conversion has been replaced by mission as outreach, with a gentler and less invasive agenda of serving those outside the church, in the hope that they might be attracted to come in, rather than compelled. The gospel is no longer being commodified and offered as a package deal with cultural or economic repercussions by missionaries from liberal churches. Some interfaith dialogue has begun in recent decades, with genuine listening and respect on both sides. Church leaders in Canada have made apologies to native communities for the abuses in the residential school system. Yet the underlying assumptions of the uniqueness of Christ and the supremacy of Christianity as the revealed way to God have not been deconstructed or renounced.

After I wrote an article several years ago for a local newspaper's religious column, in which I expressed the view that faiths other than Christianity can lead us to God and to salvation (liberation, enlightenment, wholeness), there was a flurry of sharp rebuttals from Christians who were quick to point out that the historic, biblical, orthodox tradition of Christianity upholds its uniqueness; that, in short, Jesus Christ is the *only* way, the *only* truth, the *only* door to God. "Christianity [is] exclusive and unique," wrote one pastor in a letter to me. "Every other religion [is] deceitful and false. . . . What you are proclaiming is not biblical nor is it a part of historic Christian doctrine and faith." Another pastor wrote, "Classical, historic, orthodox Christianity has always taught from the earliest days of the church that Jesus is the one mediator between man and God." "It is evident that Chaplain Reid disagrees in her column with Peter, Paul and even the Lord Jesus," reprimanded a letter to the editor. Another correspondent to the editor wrote, "If Jesus is not the only way, he is a liar, because he said, 'I am the way, the truth and the life; no man comes to the Father but by me.' If that isn't true, he is a liar." "Lucy Reid describes herself as a Christian," still another letter began, "but it seems she doesn't have much of an idea of what a Christian is or what Christianity is all about."

For several weeks the religious column and the letters page of this small paper were dominated by such rebuttals. A few readers wrote to support the views I had expressed, but, significantly, they were largely from outside the Christian mainstream. The hornets' nest I had inadvertently stirred up belongs squarely in the Christian arena. The exclusivity of Christianity as the only path to God, whether expressed violently or implied subtly, is an issue that Christians must deal with and, ultimately, renounce.

The question of the authority of the Bible is obviously central. Exclusivist texts stare out from its pages. But so too do sexist texts, proslavery texts, texts endorsing violence,[4] and plainly erroneous texts.[5] Feminists are all too aware that if we take the Bible literally we are dead in the water. Instead, we have learned to struggle with the texts, dance with them, and sometimes repudiate them, in order to set the gospel free to be good news again.

Jesus is a model for us here. He was willing to step outside the faith boundaries of his day and enlarge his own understanding of the scope of his ministry. He criticized the Pharisees most sharply for their self-righteous and judgmental excluding of others. Jesus taught that God is a bountiful giver who has no preconditions to that generosity, sending blessings to both the just and the unjust (Matt 5:45). He constantly broke through the prejudices of his culture against women, against Samaritans, and against the outcast, and told his disciples, "Whoever is not against us is for us" (Mark 9:40). The early Christians had grasped something of this inclusiveness when they broke with their Jewish roots and accepted Gentiles as equal members of the church.

Alternatives

The alternative to Christian exclusivism is not indifference or an uncritical acceptance of all religious paths as equally ethical and divinely inspired. Contrary to an uninformed secularism which maintains with a bored apathy that any religious belief is as valid as any other, it is both possible and necessary to be respectfully critical of any given belief system—including one's own. A religion that supports the practice of suttee, for instance, where a widow is burned to death on her husband's funeral pyre, must be critiqued and challenged, even as its fundamental spiritual teachings are respected. The same holds true for Christian churches that promote racism, or Muslim cultures that perpetuate female genital mutilation. A belief or practice can be rejected without dismissing the basic faith. An attitude of interfaith and cross-cultural respect does not preclude critical thought. Indeed, there is an irresponsible form of pluralism with only superficial tolerance and no desire to understand the other, or to name oppression for what it is.

Christian exclusivism need not be replaced, either, by a patronizing inclusivism that glosses over differences and wants to welcome all sincere and ethically upright believers into the Christian fold as "in effect" Christian. Roman Catholic theologian Karl Rahner, for example, developed the concept of "the anonymous Christian"—one who is seeking God and living a moral, loving, altruistic life, but who does not know Christ. Such a one might be a practicing adherent of a non-Christian religion, but is nevertheless being saved by Christ, so is a Christian who just does not know it yet.[6] Anglican bishop and author Michael Ingham describes such inclusivist efforts as "a form of theological sleight of hand" that tries to fit all of religious humanity into a Christian framework without recognizing and respecting the fundamental differences that exist between Christianity and other faiths.[7] A third route away from Christian exclusivism, one which is increasingly popular in the West today, is the path that leads to the global spiritual marketplace. Here, far from dismissing religions other than one's own as false or idolatrous, they are seized upon with delight by spiritual browsers seeking souvenir trinkets to add to their collection. The world's religions are picked over in supermarket fashion, as a smorgasbord of spiritual finger foods is accumulated for snacking upon. So the Chinese yin-yang, an ancient symbol of the paradoxical concept of eternally joined opposites, becomes an item of fashion jewelry, worn with maybe a Celtic cross and Native American dream-catcher earrings. New Age stores market this global religious paraphernalia and promote workshops and courses in practices as divergent as yoga, sweat-lodge meditation, and African drumming.

While this openness to the foreign and unfamiliar is refreshing, its commercialization and trivialization are dangerous. Removed from their spiritual and cultural context, religious symbols and practices can become hollow and superficial, and those who collect them, hopping from one to the next, are more akin to colonial travelers plundering archaeological sites than to serious spiritual seekers. Rosemary Ruether[8] warns against this form of spiritual imperialism and makes the salient point that it tends to be those from the rich (Christian) countries who are shopping around for spiritual novelties like tourists, taking what is not theirs. The process is not reciprocal, and so cannot be just. She suggests instead a more rooted, local spiritual questing, where one examines first the roots of one's own religious tradition and gathers its fruits, in a form of spiritual bioregionalism. Her caveat echoes that of Carl Jung, who in 1962 wrote: "Of what use to us is the wisdom of the Upanishads or the insight of Chinese yoga, if we desert the foundations of our own culture as though they were errors outlived and, like homeless pirates, settle with thievish intent on foreign shores?"[9]

And Yet . . .

I understand Ruether's caution and am wary of cheapening religious faith that is not native to me by co-opting pieces of it to suit my needs. Yet I also want to acknowledge with gratitude the gifts I have received from beyond my own spiritual tradition. I was invited once to speak about world religions to participants in an Anglican youth conference. Rather than describing the beliefs of the great religions, which is not my expertise and is, at any rate, a presumptuous activity for even a scholar to undertake, I chose to speak about the ways in which my own faith journey as a Christian has been enriched by gifts from other paths.

To Buddhism I owe a debt of gratitude for its teaching of mindfulness—the practice of living every moment fully awake and aware, without judgmentalism or a desire always to be in control of events. Although mindfulness is present within Christian traditions of meditation and centering prayer, it was the wise and gentle writings of Buddhist teachers such as Thich Nhat Hanh that introduced me to this way of living in the miracle of the present moment. Meditation became for me not an esoteric skill for the spiritual elite, but a lifelong practice of calming, grounding, letting go, smiling, whether in a meditation room or a traffic jam.

Another gift from the East has been yoga, which has brought me back to my body and its sacredness and wisdom after decades spent living in my thoughts or emotions. In my work I preach, teach, counsel, write, read, and pray, but my body is rarely engaged. For a body-affirming feminist this is problematic! The practice of yoga is not so much geared to attaining certain postures or flexibility; I will probably never be able to sit comfortably in the lotus position, but that is not the point. Yoga for me has become body prayer, where mind gives way to breath and spirit is incarnated in body. It celebrates the gift of physicality and heals the ancient dualistic split between body and spirit.

I have written already about the life-changing contributions of Goddess-worshiping religions to my faith. A small terra cotta figurine stands on the windowsill before me as I write, in the form of a woman sitting cross-legged and supporting on one shoulder an urn, which holds a candle. It is a symbol of the light that this path of feminine wisdom has shed for me. Similarly, in our prayer room at home we have a statue of the Buddha deep in meditation, an icon of serenity and centeredness. Neither of these symbols denies or cancels out the symbolism of the cross, central to Christianity. Instead, they remind me that I need to find within my native faith an expression and celebration of the feminine, a way of prayer that nurtures mindfulness, and a respect for the body as sacred. As Matthew Fox writes, in all authentic interfaith engagement "the result will not be to abandon one's tradition but to demand more of it."[10]

Syncretism and Creativity

Beyond a Christian exclusivism that denies the gifts of other religious paths, and beyond the multifaith consumerism that snaps up the gifts like marketplace baubles, lies the possibility of deepening our own traditions by opening doors to other ways of conceptualizing the Divine, understanding the mysteries of life, and practicing the spiritual disciplines. If this opening up can be seen as a strength and not a capitulation, and as a continued evolution of religious consciousness—a continued divine self-revelation—then the fruits can be rich. A certain humility is required, though, and Christian triumphalism and supremacism must leave by the back door.

In the past any attempt to transform Christian doctrine by the addition of other religious influences was denounced as syncretism. As Chung writes, "Syncretism has been such a 'dangerous' word for Western theologians."[11] Syncretism has been seen entirely negatively as destructive of Christian identity, sloppy, confusing, unprincipled—as a mongrel offspring. As a result, Chung observes from her own experience as an Asian Christian, "any radical break of Asian theologians from orthodoxy in an effort to dive deep into our Eastern traditions and be transformed by them has been considered suspicious by Western church leaders."[12] This in turn has hindered the development of any distinctively Asian form of Christianity—or any form other than the normative white, patriarchal model which describes itself as orthodox.

To this rigid way of defining the faith I once heard Chung offer an organic alternative. As an Asian woman whose culture includes Confucian, Buddhist, shamanic, and Christian influences, all of which have shaped her, she sees herself as one body with different parts. In a twist on the image Paul uses in 1 Cor 12 to describe the body of Christ uniting its many and varied members, Chung described herself as having a Buddhist heart, a Christian right brain, a Confucian left brain, and a shamanic gut. It was a lighthearted but clever metaphor that challenged the pompousness of Christian exclusivism and provided a deeply integrated model for a multicultural world.

With a similar lightness of touch Thich Nhat Hanh writes in *Living Buddha, Living Christ*: "Twenty years ago at a conference I attended of theologians and professors of religion, a Indian Christian friend told the assembly, 'We are going to hear about the beauties of several traditions, but that does not mean that we are going to make a fruit salad.' When it came to my turn to speak, I said, 'Fruit salad can be delicious!'"[13] A Buddhist monk, Thich Nhat Hanh describes his practice of bowing deeply before images of the Buddha and of Christ, and touching each one, before starting his meditation. This symbolizes his desire to honor the wisdom of both religious traditions, although his respect for and deep understanding of Christianity makes him no less a Buddhist. Diversity within and between religions is not a threat but a vital gift, and absolutism is a far greater danger than pluralism. "For a Buddhist to be attached to any doctrine," he explains, "even a Buddhist one, is to betray the Buddha."[14] And because human society has changed so much since the time of Jesus or the Buddha, and is continuing to change, so too religious teaching must change or become irrelevant and die.

For Thich Nhat Hanh, Jesus' statement in John's gospel, "I am the gate. Whoever enters by me will be saved" (John 10:9), is not an exclusivist assertion but a truth about the nature of his teaching: that it is a doorway into the kingdom of heaven. But, he continues, "It is said that there are 84,000 . . . doors of teaching. If you are lucky enough to find a door, it would not be very Buddhist to say that yours is the only door. In fact, we have to open even more doors for future generations."[15] Only then can our religious teaching be alive, not stale.

Because the normative Christian tradition developed in the West and was imposed upon the East by a missionary movement that had little understanding of Eastern religions or culture, Chung Hyun Kyung believes that the time has come for the spirituality of Asia to transform Christianity as we know it, and to heal some of the deep wounds of Western society. In what she sees as the dance of yin and yang, or the coming together of apparent opposites, Chung identifies certain hallmarks of Eastern spirituality that are sorely needed in the West:

the discipline of voluntary poverty as a powerful antidote to rampant consumerism;

the practice of nonattachment as a vital aspect of activism, so that it is possible, as the Tao Te Ching says, to "do your work and then step back," without burning out[16];

the soul-cleansing power of meditation, bringing inner peace with which to tackle the challenges of making outer peace in the world;

the valuing of emptiness, to balance the Christian doctrine of fullness of life and the Western sin of greed;

the understanding of the innate equilibrium and harmony between all beings in the cosmos, as a corrective to a hierarchical ordering of the universe from humans down to "lesser" creatures.[17]

Our quest or challenge is not to create a new religion based on a patchwork quilt of beliefs from this and that faith. Nor are we after a monolithic uniformity of belief according to more enlightened principles of tolerance and understanding. Rather, we are engaged in an open-ended process that is dynamic, creative, variegated, and profound. It will never be finished. No exhaustive, systematic theological book will ever be able to contain it, for the Divine cannot be contained.

Cosmic Wisdom

With the breaking down of the walls of Christian exclusivism comes an opening up to marvel at the cosmic dimension of divine revelation. As the author of Ps 139 knew, there is nowhere that the Spirit is not; in heaven, in hell, in darkness, in light, in the East, and in the West, God is present. The idea that certain peoples have privileged access to or knowledge of God shrivels up as racist arrogance under the lens of this universalist perspective. Chung in fact sees Pentecost, the Christian celebration of the coming of the Holy Spirit to the disciples, as a democratization of spirituality, where God's word no longer belongs to one race, for according to the author of the Acts of the Apostles, "All of [the disciples] were filled with the Holy Spirit, and began to speak in other languages. . . . The crowd gathered and . . . each one heard them speaking in the native language of each" (Acts 2:4, 6). This Pentecost scene is played out whenever a community finds its own language and images for the Divine, for Jesus, for sin and salvation, according to its own native culture and experience.

Similarly, Matthew Fox writes of the need for a "democratization of wisdom," whereby the wisdom deep in the heart of creation is recognized and honored in all religious traditions and in all corners of the earth, and thus is set free to bring healing, compassion, and harmony to our world.[18] Fox's universalism is theologically rooted and deeply optimistic. It lifts my spirit, in contrast to the earnest, fundamentally pessimistic theology of those Christians who believe that God has a more austere outlook on things.

Fox uses the term "Cosmic Christ" to refer to the presence of the Divine that is active throughout the universe "in every atom and galaxy. . . . [It is] the divine 'isness' present in every creature."[19] He explains that it is not an exclusively Christian term, for it has been used by non-Christians and post-Christians, and it points not to the historical Jesus but to the eternal and endlessly varied manifestations of the Divine. For Christians it is a profound and largely forgotten concept, badly in need of rediscovery. It sets Jesus in a vast context that bursts through the dam of Christian ownership. An old missionary friend of mine expressed it well when he reflected on his youthful, impassioned arrival in India to tell people about Jesus Christ, only to discover, as he learned more about the Hindu people and their spirituality, that Christ had been there long before he stepped off the boat.

So it is possible to speak of a Hindu Christ, or a Cosmic Brahman, or a Living Buddha. For its feminine overtones I love the concept of Cosmic Wisdom—Divine Sophia laughing, playing, cocreating, and leading all to drink at her well. The cosmic Holy Spirit blows where she wills; Wisdom is active throughout the universe, not only within Israel or the Christian community. And so Sophia says, "Over waves of the sea, over all the earth, and over every people and nation I have held sway" (Sir 24:6). Meister Eckhart spoke of the "great underground river" of divinity—one river, but with many wells drawing on it. This is what Fox calls deep ecumenism, and he urges: "Let the Taoists drink and the Muslims drink; let the Jews drink and the Buddhists drink; let the Christians drink and let the native peoples drink. And then tell me: What have you drunk? . . . What have you to share?"[20]

Deep ecumenism is possible when those deeply engaged in different faith traditions enter into dialogue (not debate) with one another. Superficial agreeing or one-sided preaching are equally unfruitful. There must be deeply lived faith, deep looking and deep listening, and a deep willingness to be changed and grow, if true dialogue is to occur. "That is the hope for the future," wrote Bede Griffiths, a Christian priest who spent much of his life in India, "that religions will discover their own depth. As long as they remain on their surface, they will always be divided in conflict. When they discover their depth, then we converge on the unity."[21]

Are depth and universalism feminist concepts? In the symbolism of archetypes the feminine is represented by containers, caverns, the all-embracing womb, the all-sustaining Great Mother. While the masculine separates and ranks, the feminine integrates and absorbs. In a parallel way feminism can reject the urge to create dualisms and hierarchies, and seek instead both-and solutions to either/or problems. The cut and thrust of intellectual debate has its place, as does the drive to win over, be better, surpass, or control. But we have had more than enough of the fruits of these ways in religious wars, discrimination, intolerance, and bigotry. "Know the male, yet keep to the female," advises the Tao Te Ching. "Receive the world in your arms . . . and you will be like a little child."[22]

Know the male, yet keep to the female. Know the doctrines, understand the structures, look critically at the history, and confront the obstacles, yet discover the depths, search for the unity, listen to the voiceless, embrace the outsider.

Mystical Unity and Solidarity

At the age of eighty-four Bede Griffiths suffered a stroke that he described later as the beginning of his discovery of the feminine. As a Christian priest, scholar, and monk he had been trained in the rational disciplines of his faith. "I was very masculine and patriarchal," he reflected, "and had been developing the *animus*, the left brain, all this time."[23] In the midst of the violence and confusion of the stroke, he felt a distinct call to "surrender to the Mother," and, having surrendered, he experienced a wave of total, overwhelming love. From that time on, for the remaining years of his life, he knew that he was radically changed. He opened up to the feminine, the Black Madonna, the diversity in unity, the integrating mystery that contains both order and chaos. "I think the Mother is gradually revealing itself to me and taking over," he told his biographer after the stroke. "In the last two years I have grown more than in the previous eighty-four years."[24]

Griffiths recognized that this movement from the rational and dualistic is characterized by the mystical traditions present at the heart of all religions. Mysticism, with its unitive, intuitive, deeply feminine nature, transcends or flows below the differences between religions and contains their unity. Always drawn to mysticism, his stroke opened him up to an experience of its truth at an existential level.

The breakthrough from patriarchy to the feminine has the potential to make mystics of all of us, not just elderly monks. The mystical aspect of religion is not exotic and rarified, or schismatic and dangerous, as it has sometimes been portrayed. The only danger it poses is to the structures and thinking that drive wedges between peoples and fuel fires of divisiveness and mistrust. The true mystic is deeply spiritual but sits lightly to religious dogmas and traditions. She is a person of prayer and meditation, who is naturally at home with others who practice those disciplines. She is also an activist, passionate about justice and willing to throw her lot in with oppressed peoples of any race or creed, because she knows that we are all one. Matthew Fox calls this "mystical solidarity," where we pray together and sustain political activism together—black with white, female with male, gay with straight. Chung uses the term "religious solidarity," which goes beyond a bland religious pluralism and through interreligious dialogue to a revolutionary common struggle against exclusivity.

Mysticism that is not rooted in compassion and fruitful in justice is artificial. It may look holy and sound spiritual, but it is a sham, ungrounded and self-indulgent. For this reason the great mystics in history, such as Meister Eckhart, Teresa of Avila, and Mohandas Gandhi, have always been reformers very much engaged in the issues of their day. Their deep understanding of the unity of all led them to challenge the structures that divide. So mysticism is also inherently prophetic, speaking the truth about injustice and naming the evils that corrupt and disfigure God's creation. As a result, many mystics have been killed, silenced, or otherwise rejected by the powers that be—as Jesus himself was, the Christian mystic par excellence.

In comparison with the inclusive wisdom of mysticism, much of what passes for religious activity is shallow and parochial. Church synods debate their budgets with passion and wring their hands about declining membership, but have little to say and less to do for the poor outside their walls. Ecumenical committees discuss the finer points of theology and produce dry position statements, but the faith communities they represent continue to regard each other with suspicion and prejudice. Of course, religious housekeeping and theologizing are necessary, but if we forget "the great underground river" that feeds all our puny wells, or if we begin to believe that we alone know the truth, or if we concentrate our energies introspectively, then we are, in Fox's words, "boring our young, killing our souls, trivializing our worship, and exterminating the planet."[25]

The Sway of the Elephant

Sometimes the folly of our narrow-mindedness is laughable, and humor is the most effective way to highlight and deflate it. "I have felt the swaying of the elephant's shoulders," wrote the sixteenth-century Hindu mystic Mirabai, "and you want me to climb on a jackass? Try to be serious!"[26]

The sway of the elephant is the magnificent, awe-inspiring presence of the Divine in our midst, and one who has felt it, even once, realizes how paltry and partial are our human attempts to define or contain it, much less claim exclusive truth about it. How preposterous, then, to insist that the rider dismount and settle for a donkey.

Yet in the controversy surrounding my newspaper article, when conservative Christians in the community were denouncing me as heretical and some were attempting to have my ministry curtailed, the feelings of hurt I experienced eroded my faith and pushed me back to the anxiety and self-doubt I had felt as a teenager when my evangelical friends had told me that my liberal beliefs were unacceptable. It is difficult to be in Christian ministry while being told that one is not really a Christian.

One of the strongest opponents to my views came to see me, ostensibly to listen to me in order to understand me better. What followed was a long and one-sided harangue, where he repeatedly told me that I was promoting false doctrine, was not a Christian, had a rebellious spirit, had been led gravely astray by worldly views and the devil, and was leading others into error. At the end of our appointment I stood up to go, but he continued pressing his point home even as I walked to the elevator. Finally he said, "Lucy, I would like to say 'God bless you,' but I'm afraid I can't. I can only pray that God will have mercy on you." As the elevator doors slid open and I gratefully stepped inside, I said (with a good deal more bravado that I felt), "I'm sure she will." But for the rest of the day I shook, with a sense of having been physically attacked. And as the subsequent days and weeks passed, the weight of this condemnation grew more burdensome and undermining.

Healing and groundedness came for me through an active imagination meditation my spiritual director suggested. Christmas was approaching; the controversy had chewed through several months. Jean directed me to spend some time in prayer imagining that I was hosting a Christmas party to which my critics were invited, along with Jesus and anyone else whom my imagination might spontaneously include. She suggested I ask each of them, in the course of the meditation, how I should prepare for Christmas. The result was profoundly illuminating. I recorded it in my journal like this:

> The guests begin to arrive at my home. First come four of those who have criticized my universalism as heretical, including three who have tried to have funding withdrawn from my chaplaincy ministry. I welcome them with as much grace as I can muster, but I feel very uncomfortable. The house already seems full and dangerous. I'm nervous and on edge. But the doorbell rings again, and Jesus is there. Behind him, small and beaming, is Thich Nhat Hanh. I feel tremendous relief.
>
> Leaving the door open in case other guests arrive, I go around the room offering people food and drinks. Then I ask each one how I should prepare best for Christmas.
>
> The first critic says, "I'm so glad you asked me that. I'm going to tell you. To prepare for Christmas you must get down on your knees and humble yourself. You are not worthy, but God is gracious. Pray that he will forgive your disobedient heart."
>
> The second critic says, "I've been praying so hard for you. If only you would stop questioning and just believe. Prepare to meet Jesus by welcoming him into your heart as King of kings and Lord of lords."
>
> The third critic says, "You are a good person, but that's not enough, is it? You don't really know Jesus as your personal Lord and Savior. Christmas will be empty for you unless you turn to Jesus and accept him as your Savior. Put away your pride."
>
> The fourth critic says, "You are a dangerous woman. I'm leaving." And he exits. I feel agitated, threatened, and, above all, unsure of myself.
>
> Then a friend and former colleague appears on the scene, having let himself in. He says, "Your beliefs are often different from mine, and sometimes they startle me. But they're life giving. They reveal God to people in new ways. To prepare for Christmas, celebrate the ways you do know God and do encounter Jesus."

And now Jesus approaches. He is smiling warmly and gently. I feel enormously reassured and loved. He says, "Can you hear the good news? Can you separate it out from the bad? You know my voice—just trust it. Let go of what isn't helpful. Trust your Yeses and get to know them better. You and I worked hard to find them and say them."

All this time Thich Nhat Hanh has been sitting cross-legged on the floor by the coffee table, watching us and smiling. I know he thinks we're making heavy weather of something very simple. Jesus goes and sits with him. The critics are talking earnestly together at the other end of the long room.

For a moment I'm not sure where I ought to be, as hostess. But I know where I want to be. So I pass more food and drink around to everyone, and I thank them all for coming, then I sit down with Jesus and Thich Nhat Hanh. The three of us are laughing.

I have felt the sway of the elephant; I have found the Divine in myself, in Eastern wisdom, in the earth, in the darkness. And you want me to ride on a jackass? To nail the Cosmic Christ onto the structures of Christendom? To domesticate Sophia's wild voice and paint over the whole canvas of the human search for God with one uniform color? Try to be serious!

Swimming, Flying, Digging in the Compost

The result of choosing not to paint by numbers, not to color within the lines, is the ability to take responsibility for one's own spiritual life. It requires growing up. And surely this is one of the goals in the journey of faith—to put away childish things such as black and white thinking, the desire for parental approval, the dependence on authority figures, and instead to make the heroic journey, which is ultimately a solitary one.

For Christians, the church and its traditions and doctrines have often been regarded as a means of transportation in the journey of faith—the ark of salvation gathering all on board and bound for the shores of heaven. In this model, baptism is a ticket that guarantees a berth, the captain and crew are the ordained clergy, and the theologians navigate safe passage through the rocks and storms around. Passengers may be entirely inactive, sleeping in their deck chairs, or they may be more engaged in the tasks and process of the voyage. But they imperil their lives if they attempt to leave the ship. Tales are told of the dreadful fates that overtook those who fell or jumped overboard. Yet God calls us to learn to swim. Getting off the boat is a frightening necessity.

Some are pushed off. Like Jonah they become undesirable on board and are thrown into the waves with labels such as heretic, feminist, pervert, pagan. Others fall when storms send the boat reeling and the railings cannot contain the staggering passengers. A personal tragedy often precipitates such a fall, when faith breaks down and proves flimsy or rusted through. Most of the church alumni whom I meet have either fallen or been pushed off the good ship. Some disembarked after having discovered that the ship was still moored in a safe haven, going nowhere. But once off, it becomes possible to enter the water and learn the mysteries of its buoyancy, its potency, its depth, and the life it sustains within it.

I see the great spiritual leaders of our faith as those who not only rocked the boat but learned to dive, to float, to row, to kayak, to raft, to dog-paddle, even to walk on water. And like Jesus calling Peter to get out of the safety of the boat and join him on the water (Matt 14:22–33), the prophets of our day urge us to do the same. There is a time to be carried and a time to dive in; a time for community and a time for the heroine's journey alone; a time to follow instructions and a time to say No.

My journey, often very gingerly undertaken, has led me past the point of security. And I am deeply grateful for that. The frustrations, injustices, doubts, and conflicts I have encountered have pushed me over the side repeatedly and into a place where I know I am alive and encompassed by God, the One in whom we live and move and have our being. I still love the ship, but I cannot allow it to make my journey for me. Orthodoxy is too high a price to pay. Besides, the ocean is too inviting. The Unitarians who first heard these thoughts in their embryonic form at a conference assured me that I was one of them—a closet Unitarian, beginning to come out. Certainly writing this book has been a form of coming out for me, as I have faced and told the truth about my faith as a feminist. But my roots remain Christian, and as I demand more of my Christian tradition so I find places where it rises to the challenge and people who have redefined Christianity beyond the straitjacket of patriarchal orthodoxy.

Some years ago, during a feminist spirituality conference, I encountered the newly coined and lighthearted term "compost-Christian." Unlike a post-Christian, who has abandoned Christianity all together, a compost-Christian has thrown out the rubbish, cut out the rotten pieces, peeled off the tough skins, cracked open the shells, and recycled the whole organic heap. At first it stinks. But over time, with digging and turning, the miracle of decomposition begins. In the dark, with enough warmth and a little worm activity, a rich loamy soil is created that is capable of sustaining new life.

So I am a compost-Christian, very different from the pious Anglo-Catholic teenager who admired her parish priest so much that she wanted to be just like him. I am deeply grateful now that the Church of England was so resistant for so long to the ordination of women, because meanwhile I had some exploring to do. Initially I was thrust upon the journey; it was not of my choosing. But I have come to see it as a blessing and a growth opportunity that continue to change me. It led me to discover the feminine face of God and the history and powerful mythology of the

Goddess. It forced me to hammer out my theology on the anvil of my experience, and to dare to disagree with the theological orthodoxies of the day. It brought me not into the promised land of ordination into the status quo but into the sacred wilderness of letting go and transformation. And it gave me a glimpse of the holy oneness-in-diversity of all that is—the interconnectedness of life and the omnipresence of the Divine.

It has been a feminist journey of faith. I am grateful to the women who walked it ahead of me and left signs along the way, and to those who have walked parts of it with me. I am grateful, too, to those men who have shared the journey—especially David, my life companion. Above all I am grateful to God, to Divine Sophia, with her cosmic wisdom and dancing step. She changes everything.

CREDO

I believe in you, Holy One,
Womb of creation,
Mother and Father of us all.
In you we live
and move
and have our being.

I trust in your compassionate love
flowing through the universe,
taking human form in Jesus
and calling us to wholeness.

I believe in your renewing Spirit,
who broods over chaos,
brings forth life,
and leads her dance in the wilderness.

And I stand before your call to justice,
I labor with you for the birth of compassion
And I open my heart
to enter
the ocean
of you.

Notes

1. Julian of Norwich, *Showings* (ed. E. Colledge, J. Walsh, and J. Leclercq; New York: Paulist Press, 1978), 259.

2. Mary Daly, *Beyond God the Father* (Boston: Beacon, 1973), 165.

3. Chung Hyun Kyung, *Struggle to be the Sun Again* (Maryknoll, N.Y.: Orbis Books, 1994).

4. See Phyllis Trible, *Texts of Terror: Literary-Feminist Readings of Biblical Narratives* (Philadelphia: Fortress, 1984).

5. See, e.g., Josh 10:12–13, where it is assumed that the sun revolves around the earth.

6. See Karl Rahner, "Christianity and the Non-Christian Religions," in *Theological Investigations* (vol. 5; Baltimore: Helicon, 1966), 115–34.

7. Michael Ingham, *Mansions of the Spirit* (Toronto: Anglican Book Centre, 1997), 71.

8. Address given at the University of Waterloo, Ontario, Canada, October 13, 1994.

9. Quoted in Matthew Fox, *The Coming of the Cosmic Christ* (San Francisco: HarperSanFrancisco, 1988), 243.

10. Fox, *Coming of the Cosmic Christ*, 236.

11. Kyung, *Struggle to be the Sun Again*, 113.

12. Ibid.

13. Thich Nhat Hanh, *Living Buddha, Living Christ* (New York: Riverhead Books, 1995), 1.

14. Ibid., 55.

15. Ibid., 39.

16. *Tao Te Ching* (trans. Stephen Mitchell; New York: Harper and Row, 1988), 9.

17. Chung Hyun Kyung, conference on "Asian Eco-Feminist Liberation Theology," Paris, Ontario, June 1997.

18. Fox, *Coming of the Cosmic Christ*, 240.

19. Ibid., 241–42.

20. Ibid., 244.

21. *A Human Search: Bede Griffiths Reflects on His Life* (ed. John Swindells; Liguori, Mo.: Triumph Books, 1997), 94.

22. *Tao Te Ching*, 28.

23. *Human Search*, 89.

24. Ibid., 98, 102.

25. Fox, *Coming of the Cosmic Christ*, 228.

26. Quoted in *Women in Praise of the Sacred* (ed. Jane Hirshfield; New York: HarperCollins, 1995), 139.

CHAPTER 8
Prayers for the Pilgrimage

A PSALM OF GOD'S CREATING LOVE

In the beginning
there was a Mother

And her womb contained life
variety
possibility

And she knew that it was good

In the beginning
there was a birthing
of life from Life
of many from One

God gave birth to the world
She pushed and gasped
She bled and tore
So much pain, so much love

And God delivered us
in her labor of love—
naked, vulnerable
flesh of her flesh

And God saw herself in our eyes
Her grace in our bodies
Her love in our hearts
And she cherished her children

In the beginning
there was a Mother
who gave herself as food—
tenderly, tenderly—
at one with her children

We are beloved
We are beloved now
and ever shall be
as it was in the beginning

A PSALM TO THE GODDESS

Goddess
(forbidden word)
in the cavern of my soul
I search for you.
You are a whispered rumor
of someone I once knew;
a story told between the lines;
a shadow in the ruins.

Did I imagine you
or forget you?

Goddess
(pagan idol)
without you
my soul is a one-winged bird.
Your memory haunts me.
I see your face in my mirror.

Goddess
(dangerous heresy)

you are chaos and wisdom,
spirit and womb,
earth and universe.

You are life,
you are all,
you are One.

Goddess,
Ancient Mother,
return.

A PSALM OF MOURNING (FROM PSALM 42)

As a deer longs for flowing streams,
so my soul longs for you, Birth Mother, Earth Mother.
My soul thirsts for you,
the Goddess of Life.
When will I find you?

I weep like a motherless child,
while people say to me,
"There is no Goddess."
Why did they banish you?
When did we choose oppression and violence?

I am a heretic.
My foremothers were murdered as witches.
Abuse kills my sisters' souls
like a deadly wound.

I am bereft.
I am afraid.

But I remember—
or I imagine—
a time when there was dancing and prayer to you;
a time when women's bodies were sacred;
a time when armies were unknown.

Why am I bereft?
Why do I fear?
I turn to you, eternal Mother,
my life and my source.

My heart is sinking,
desolation howls around me.
I miss you.
So I remember,
I invent,
I recreate.

I am held upon the deep waters of your love,
sustained within the womb of your compassion.

Day by day
your embrace surrounds me
and at night your song is with me,
a prayer to the Goddess of life.

Birth Mother, Earth Mother,
come
and bring us home.

A PSALM OF GOD'S ETERNAL PRESENCE (FROM PSALM 139)

O God, you have searched me and known me.
You know when I weep and when I laugh.
You understand me completely—
my thoughts, my fears, my intentions.

While I grope for words
and search for myself
you hold me in the palm of your hand.

Where could I go that you are not?
How could I ever be apart from you?
For you are in heaven and hell,
in east and west,
in darkness and light.

When I fall in love
you are there.
When my heart breaks
you catch my tears and speak my name.
When I cradle my child at my breast
or mourn at the graveside of death
you are with me,
holding me,
closer than breathing.

If I say, "My faith is gone. There is no God!"
you still believe in me
and you guide me through the night.

You made me in your own image,
formed me in your womb.
You saw who I could become
and gave me a lifetime to understand.

How magnificent is the mystery that you are!
You encompass all that is
and yet you beat within my heart.

Fill me, O Spirit of life;
transform me into myself, your Self.
And lead me in the ancient way of wisdom.

A PSALM ON THE LOSS OF FAITH

Holy One,
I ask for the courage to doubt:
to paddle my boat
down the river of disbelief
to the ocean of a deeper faith

Teach me to let go;
deliver me from dead certainties

Let doubt be the tooth
that cracks open the shell,

the rock on which to shed
a skin of constriction

When belief dies
and faith lies cold
may I sing a requiem
of Alleluias
and plant a crocus
on the grave

MAGNIFICAT

My soul is pregnant with joy
O God my love, O God my life
My body and spirit leap and sing
For your liberating word is Yes!

Now I can hold my head up
Now I can stand without shame
Your Yes to me has healed me
set me free
I am blessed beyond imagination

Your love is constant
aching for us
calling us back
lifting us up

You overturn our unjust powers
naming the poor blessed
the rich empty

You burst into our prisons
and dance us free
You topple our pompous thrones
and deliver us from ourselves

Your promise is freedom
Your gift is liberation
Your grace is wholeness

I am in you, encompassing God
And you are in me, Divine Child
of abundant life

My soul is pregnant with joy
and you will deliver me

A WILDERNESS PSALM

Out of the depths I cry to you,
Grandmother God.
Out of the darkness I call.

I am bereft and alone:
a refugee from my own home,
estranged from my own people.

I walk in the valley
of the shadow of death.
I am a nomad
in the wilderness.

My prayer falls like a rock
to the ground.
Your presence eludes me.

But it was you who called me here.
You spoke my name and wooed me out.

You showed me the wisdom of the night
and sang the song of silence
to my heart.

Crone of the darkness
come to me.
You hold my life
in your old woman hands.

Grandmother God
walk with me.

For I cannot go back
to that city of light.

A PSALM TO GAIA GOD

Gaia, Spirit of life,
come to us!
We have forgotten who we are:
claiming power and dominion
we have named ourselves
masters of Nature.
Call us your children
and show us our place in the web.

Gaia, Mother of all,
come to us!
We have severed your creation:
we have ranked and exploited,
divided and conquered.
Humble us, heal us, help us,
and bring us back to earth.

Gaia, spiralling dancer,
come to us!
We have feared our mortality:
we have used death as a weapon
and made heaven our escape.
Teach us the gentle steps of letting go
and guide us to the wonder
of heaven on earth.

Gaia, Holy Oneness,
come to us!
You are all we have:
you are in all life
and all life is in you.
Lead us home to ourselves,
home to you
and home to all that is,
for earth's sake.
Amen.

A PSALM OF BLESSING

Blessed are you, Breath of the universe,
Great cosmic Spirit, blessed are you.
Blessed are you for the pulse of creation;
Glory to you, Holy One within all.

Blessed are you, Wisdom of ages,
Our souls' inspiration, blessed are you.
Blessed are you for all teachers and prophets;
Glory to you, Holy One within all.

Blessed are you, divine underground river,
Flowing beneath us, blessed are you.
Blessed are you for the wellsprings of insight;
Glory to you, Holy One within all.

Blessed are you, Word of compassion,
Enfleshed in your creatures, blessed are you.
Blessed are you for your infinite voices,
Glory to you, Holy One within all.

Blessed are you, beyond our comprehension,
In clouds of unknowing, blessed are you.
Blessed are you for surpassing our dogmas;
Glory to you, Holy One within all.

AN INVOCATION

We call upon our Mother the Earth
to ground us
to root us
to calm us and nourish us

We call upon the Divine Spirit
to inspire us
to energize us
to flow between us

We call upon Holy Wisdom
to teach us
to challenge us
to weave the strands of our lives
into beauty and purpose

Come into our midst
Gaia, Ruach, Sophia
And bless us with roots, wings, and wisdom

A MANTRA

O God, I am held upon the deep waters of your love
O Christ, I am planted in the rich earth of your passion
Sophia, I am dancing in your circle
Holy Spirit, I am a feather on your breath

THE PRAYER OF JESUS

Our Father, Mother, Breath of life,
Open our hearts to love.
Your Holy Spirit come upon us;
Your way be lived by all creation.
Give us today our food for the journey.
Forgive us our sins
And teach us to release others from the prisons of our hearts.
Walk beside us through our trials,
And dissolve the evil within us.
For you are love and life and mystery,
Now and forever.
Amen.

PRAYERS OF PETITION

In peace let us pray
to the God of our hearts

(Silence)

In the pain of the world
In violence and destruction
In injustice and danger
OPEN OUR HEARTS TO COMPASSION

In the darkness of death
In despair and isolation
In sorrow and loss
OPEN OUR SOULS TO HEALING

In the summons to care
In work and in action
In challenge and calling
OPEN OUR WILLS TO COURAGE

In the sunshine of joy
In love and in passion
In contentment and peace
OPEN OUR SPIRITS TO GRATITUDE

O God ever present
Within us, around us
Cradle our lives
In the palm of your hand.
AMEN

A BLESSING

The love of the Holy One
Enfold you
The labor of the Birthing One
Deliver you
The wisdom of the Wild One
Transform you
The peace of the All in One
Sustain you
And bless you
And guide you home
Amen

SELECT BIBLIOGRAPHY

Altizer, Thomas J. J., ed. *Toward a New Christianity*. New York: Harcourt, Brace and World, 1967.

Artress, Lauren. *Walking a Sacred Path: The Labyrinth as a Spiritual Tool*. New York: Riverhead Books, 1995.

Ashe, Geoffrey. *The Virgin*. London: Routledge and Kegan Paul, 1976.

Beauvoir, Simone de. *The Second Sex*. Translated by H. M. Parshley. London: Penguin, 1983.

Bloesch, Donald G. *Is the Bible Sexist?* Westchester, Ill.: Crossway Books, 1982.

Borg, Marcus. *The God We Never Knew*. San Francisco: HarperSanFrancisco, 1997.

Brown, Joanne Carlson, and Rebecca Parker. *Christianity, Patriarchy, and Abuse*. Cleveland: Pilgrim, 1989.

Chervin, Ronda, and Mary Neill. *Bringing the Mother with You*. New York: Seabury, 1982.

Chödrön, Pema. *The Wisdom of No Escape*. Boston: Shambhala Publications, 1991.

Christ, Carol P. *Diving Deep and Surfacing: Women Writers on Spiritual Quest*. Boston: Beacon, 1980.

Christ, Carol P., and Judith Plaskow, eds. *Womanspirit Rising*. San Francisco: Harper Collins, 1992.

Chung Hyun Kyung. *Struggle to be the Sun Again*. Maryknoll, N.Y.: Orbis, 1990.

Clark, Elizabeth and Herbert Richardson, ed., *Women and Religion: The Original Sourcebook of Women in Christian Thought*. San Francisco: Harper and Row, 1977.

Daly, Mary. *Beyond God the Father*. Boston: Beacon, 1973.

Diamond, Irene, and Gloria Feman Orenstein, eds. *Reweaving the World: The Emergence of Ecofeminism*. San Francisco: Sierra Club Books, 1990.

Eisler, Riane. *The Chalice and the Blade*. New York: Harper and Row, 1987.

Fowler, James. *Weaving a New Creation*. New York: HarperCollins, 1991.

Fox, Matthew. *The Coming of the Cosmic Christ*. San Francisco: HarperSanFrancisco, 1988.

———. *Creation Spirituality*. San Francisco: HarperSanFrancisco, 1991.

———. ed. *Meditations with Meister Eckhart*. Santa Fe, N.M.: Bear and Co., 1983.

———. *Original Blessing*. Santa Fe, N.M.: Bear and Co., 1983.

———. *Whee! We, Wee All the Way Home*. Gaithersburg, Md.: Consortium Books, 1976.

Gateley, Edwina. *A Warm, Moist, Salty God: Women Journeying towards Wisdom*. Trabuco Canyon, Calif.: Source Books, 1993.

Goldenberg, Naomi. *Changing of the Gods*. Boston: Beacon, 1979.

Greeley, A. M. *The Mary Myth: On the Femininity of God*. New York: Seabury, 1977.

Haughton, Rosemary. *The Passionate God*. New York: Paulist Press, 1981.

Hirshfield, Jane, ed. *Women in Praise of the Sacred*. New York: HarperCollins, 1995.

Ingham, Michael. *Mansions of the Spirit*. Toronto: Anglican Book Centre, 1997.

Julian of Norwich. *Showings*. Translated by Edmund Colledge and James Walsh. New York: Paulist Press, 1978.

McFague, Sallie. *Metaphorical Theology*. London: SCM Press, 1983.

Maitland, Sara. *A Map of the New Country*. London: Routledge and Kegan Paul, 1983.

Mitchell, J., ed. *The God I Want*. London: Constable, 1967.

Moltmann-Wendel, Elisabeth, and Jürgen Moltmann. *Humanity in God*. London: SCM Press, 1983.

Nhat Hanh, Thich. *Living Buddha, Living Christ*. New York: Riverhead Books, 1995.

Neumann, Erich. *The Great Mother*. Translated by Ralph Manheim. Princeton, N.J.: Bollingen, 1974.

Oliver, Mary. *Dream Work*. New York: Atlantic Monthly Press, 1986.

Pagels, Elaine. *The Gnostic Gospels*. Middlesex, England: Weidenfeld and Nicolson, 1980.

Parvey, Constance, ed. *The Community of Women and Men in the Church*. Geneva: World Council of Churches, 1983.

Pittenger, Norman. *The Lure of Divine Love*. New York: Pilgrim, 1979.

Rabuzzi, Kathryn Allen. *The Sacred and the Feminine: Toward a Theology of Housework*. New York: Seabury, 1982.

Roberts, Elizabeth, and Elias Amidon, eds. *Earth Prayers*. San Francisco: HarperSanFrancisco, 1991.

Ruether, Rosemary Radford. *Gaia and God*. San Francisco: HarperSanFrancisco, 1992.

———. *Mary, the Feminine Face of the Church*. London: SCM Press, 1979.

———. *New Woman/New Earth*. New York: Seabury, 1975.

———. ed. *Religion and Sexism*. New York: Simon and Schuster, 1974.

———. *Sexism and God-Talk*. London: SCM Press, 1983.

———. *Women-Church: Theology and Practice of Feminist Liturgical Communities*. San Francisco: Harper and Row, 1986.

Sjoo, Monica, and Barbara Mor. *The Great Cosmic Mother: Rediscovering the Religion of the Earth*. San Francisco: HarperSanFrancisco, 1987.

Sölle, Dorothee. *The Strength of the Weak*. Philadelphia: Westminster, 1984.

Starhawk. *The Fifth Sacred Thing*. New York: Bantam, 1993.

———. *The Spiral Dance: The Rebirth of the Ancient Religion of the Goddess*. New York: Harper and Row, 1979.

Stone, Merlin. *When God Was a Woman*. San Diego: Harvest/Harcourt Brace, 1976.

Swindells, John, ed. *A Human Search: Bede Griffiths Reflects on His Life*. Liguori, Mo.: Triumph Books, 1997

Tao Te Ching. Translated by Stephen Mitchell. New York: Harper and Row, 1988.

Thouless, R. H. *The Lady Julian*. London: SPCK, 1924.

Trible, Phyllis. *Texts of Terror: Literary-Feminist Readings of Biblical Narratives*. Philadelphia: Fortress, 1984.

Uhlein, Gabriele, ed. *Meditations with Hildegard of Bingen*. Santa Fe, N.M.: Bear and Co., 1983.

Waal, Esther de. *God under my Roof*. Oxford: SLG Press, 1984.

Walker, Alice. *The Color Purple*. New York: Pocket Books, 1982.

Warner, Marina. *Alone of All Her Sex*. London: Weidenfeld and Nicolson, 1976.

Woman's Guild/Panel on Doctrine, Church of Scotland. *The Motherhood of God*. Edited by Alan E. Lewis. Edinburgh: St. Andrew Press, 1984.

Woodman, Marion. *The Pregnant Virgin*. Toronto: Inner City Books, 1985.

Woodman, Marion, with Jill Mellick. *Coming Home to Myself*. Berkeley, Calif.: Conari Press, 1998.

Woodruff, Sue. *Meditations with Mechtild of Magdeburg*. Sante Fe, N.M.: Bear and Co., 1982.

Young, Frances. *Can These Dry Bones Live?* London: SCM Press, 1982.

Zappone, Katherine. *The Hope for Wholeness: A Spirituality for Feminists*. Mystic, Conn.: Twenty-Third Publications, 1991.

INDEX